Make Time for Yourself –
It's Your Time

Make Time for Yourself – It's Your Time

Abbot Primate Notker Wolf

Translated by
Gerlinde Büchinger-Schmid

Edited by
Sue Bollans

Cataloguing in Publication Data — DK
[Courtesy: D.K. Agencies (P) Ltd. <docinfo@dkagencies.com>]

Wolf, Abbot Primate Notker.
Make time for yourself : it's your time / Abbot Primate Notker Wolf ; translated by Gerlinde Büchinger-Schmid ; edited by Sue Bollans.
p. cm.
ISBN 13: 9788124605592
ISBN 10: 8124605599

1. Time management – Religious aspects – Christianity. 2. Time in the Bible. 3. Christian life. I. Büchinger-Schmid, Gerlinde. II. Bollans, Sue. III. Title.

DDC 248.4 22

ISBN 13: 978-81-246-0559-2 ISBN 10: 81-246-0559-9

First published in Germany in 2009

Second edition published in 2009

English translation published in India in 2010

Published and printed by:
D.K. Printworld (P) Ltd.
Regd. office : '*Srikunj*,' F-52, Bali Nagar
Ramesh Nagar Metro Station
New Delhi – 110 015-13
Phones : (011) 2545 3975; 2546 6019; *Fax* : (011) 2546 5926
E-mail : indology@dkprintworld.com
Web : www.dkprintworld.com

Preface

RECENTLY at the airport in Rome, the young woman at the check-in for the flight to Santo Domingo and Guatemala looked at me as she gave me back my documents and said in disbelief: "You are in the air more than a pilot!" And it's true that I do cover a lot of miles every year.

I am sure that three of the ten days of my trip to Santo Domingo and Guatemala were spent sitting in a plane. And in addition, nearly every day I travelled for two to four hours by car.

My mobile existence might seem extreme, but this is the general tendency today. It has to do with the increase in mobility and the networking of our world, and in my case of course with my function: as an Abbot Primate I am responsible for 800 monasteries, which are located on all five of the world's continents. To fulfil my responsibilities I sometimes have to live the life of a manager with an improbable number of appointments. And on the other hand, my life as a monk is ordered in an entirely different way.

The question preoccupying many people today concerns me too: with all the stress and hectic pace of modern life, can you still find some peace? With all the pressure on you from outside, can you still be in control of your own time?

An international manager who recently sat next to me on the plane asked, "You're so calm, even though your situation is basically no different from ours. How do you do it?"

It was this question that prompted me to start writing. My idea was that people might be particularly interested in reading about the thoughts and experiences of someone who is himself working under great time pressure.

Sometimes when I mentioned what I was writing about, people asked with a touch of irony whether I was going to practise what I preached. I told them, "I believe that what I have in common with others is not only a specific need but also the fact that I am looking for ways to deal with it. But what I believe in particular is that the tradition I come from is very helpful in this respect."

Many people, not only managers, suffer from having less and less time for the things that are really important. Time for yourself – this seems to be becoming a scarce luxury good.

"Time for myself " is time to be together with others or to be free for prayer. I can simply drop my work. This for me is very important: just to stop what I am doing and say now something else is more important. During prayer it is God, during conversation it is the other person.

The ancient proverb of Qohelet in the Bible is as true today as it ever was: "Everything in life has its own time."

There is a time of joy and also a time of sadness. A person who is under such time pressure that he cannot let go in order to cry is in a critical state. And so is a person who cannot laugh heartily.

I am repeatedly guided by the wisdom of this preacher from the Old Testament. Of course I cannot separate the periods of joy and sadness as I would like to do. They are going to overlap. But it is not just a question of dividing up an objective span of time. It is a question of humanizing this time.

The time I spend with other people or in a one-to-one conversation is quite different from the time when I am trying to see how many e-mails I ought to get done in an hour. During a conversation I am not looking at my watch, there is no rush. A *person* is there and it is *his* time. This applies even more to prayer. Then time acquires not only a human but a divine dimension.

Even Jesus is a shining example of how to make use of time. Over and over again he sought solitude in order to pray. And when he walked by the Sea of Nazareth with his disciples he devoted his time solely to them. The story of the road to Emmaus illustrates how he was there for people who were close to him and wanted to tell him their troubles. But even the disciples still sometimes had to wait if other people needed his help. I love these stories, also those that relate how Jesus withdrew, exhausted, to the home of his friends in Bethany, where he himself could simply become "human" again in the literal sense of the word. Jesus also set limits when others, such as the Pharisees, tried to put pressure on him or importune him. As we read in the gospel of Saint Luke, he also rebuffed somebody who was acting as if his life would never come to an end. He told a parable in which God says to a rich man: "You fool! This very night the demand will be made for your soul; and this hoard of yours, whose will it be then? (Luke 12:20)

I am also guided by our founder St Benedict. Based on his reflections on the quality of time, the founder of western monasticism succeeded as virtually no other has done in creating a highly refined way of structuring time. The daily routine of the monks, which is balanced and governed by an inner rhythm based on the liturgy and nature and gives each day and year a special quality, still has much that can serve as a source of inspiration and benefit for the secular world today.

The time which is the subject of this book is nothing that we can "have" or "take," nothing we can trade or with which we can become rich. Some people say "time is money." And it is certainly right that time is precious. Because it is limited. Our lifetime, like our life, cannot be bought, it is a gift. When we say we are giving each other time or talk about "time costs," then it is clear from the language how precious time is.

Of course there is the time which is measured by the clock in minutes and seconds. This is important too, because it gives order to our lives. But this order is only half of life. Our lives are finite. And when we talk about time, we are also talking about the art of making good and sensible use of our lives during the limited time we are in the world. Those who want to save time and constantly become more hectic may well end up by losing time.

A general return to slowness is no remedy. We cannot isolate ourselves from the tempo of our world, but in the midst of this pressure must look for ways of finding "our" time. Life requires time. And if I don't take any time for myself any more, then this life is not worth anything.

There is apparently a valley in the Tyrol where people greet each other with "Take your time!" And even if someone has made this up, there is something in this greeting. It is almost a blessing.

To take your time, to take time for yourself, to make more conscious use of your time – this is what this book is about: Make time for yourself. It's your time!

So at the end of our lives we can leave the temporal world in a state of blessedness.

Contents

1 Born for Joy

In 1979 a group of Japanese Buddhists and Shintoists visited my monastery in St Ottilien. The monks stayed with us for some time and shared our daily routine. Before they left, journalists came to interview them. Their first question was, "What struck you most about the monastery?" I was very curious to hear what our guests from Asia would say. And what they said was "Joy"!

My spontaneous reaction was, if only Nietzsche could have heard that!

I am convinced that Christianity needs more morals and less moralizing. Nietzsche's stipulation that "Christians should look more joyful" is still valid today.

Our destiny is happiness and joy and not suffering and misfortune. Nobody, when asked what he is born for, will say "to be sorrowful." Fullness, and also joy in fullness is what life is about. Jesus said, "I want that they may have life in fullness – and still joy in fullness." What this means is real joy and not the apparent joy promised us by advertisements. Jesus' basic feeling is joy in life. This joy, which comes from God, is one way of getting to know God. This is the essence of his message: "that my joy may be in you and that your joy may be complete" (Joh.15:11).

We were thus certainly not born to be fearful. In the past, life in the monasteries and everyday Christian morals were often characterized by control. This gave rise to anxiety. Looking back on this now, it seems rather infantile, with obedience interpreted as submissiveness or the two confused with one another.

The monastic tradition has quite different points of reference. "How long will you pay attention to all the others and not to yourself?" Yes indeed, how can someone who treats himself badly be good to anyone else? So think about "giving yourself to yourself," as recommended by Bernhard of Clairvaux. He wrote this in the twelfth century in a letter to his pupil Bernardo da Pisa, the monk who was later to become Pope Eugen III. As important as the office of pope is, as massive and varied the responsibilities, as heavy the burden, he nevertheless advises Bernardo not only to devote his time to others, but to make sure he does not neglect his own life. Bernhard knew the strengths and weaknesses of man. Deeply rooted in the spirituality of the Benedictines, he was aware of the necessity and the purpose of an ascetic way of life. But for this saint, godliness and humanitarianism belong together.

To indulge in something is the sign of a big heart, generosity and joy in life which has a communicative, benevolent character and does not exclude others.

We only have one life and it is precious. We are sharing the richness of existence.

Who knows how long we will be in this world . . .

For all of us life is finite.

So it is right to say, "Live accordingly!"

Horace says "Carpe diem" – seize the day! Seize the day before it vanishes. Make use of opportunities while there is time. Goethe refers to finiteness with the words "Ah, linger on, thou art so fair!" Time is fleeting – this is a view reflected throughout the history of wisdom. But this does not have to mean withdrawal from the world, quite the contrary.

Turning towards finiteness – which also means turning towards death – can lead you back into life. "Make good use of every opportunity you have" (Ephesians 5:16). This text is used on Laetare Sunday, sung to a beautiful choral melody, and, in the middle of Lent, it looks ahead to the joy of Easter. The meaning of the word laetare is a motto for life. "Rejoice in the Lord always."

The person who opens himself to joy, grants himself joy and gives space and time in his life to it, will have a big heart. This is what is behind Bernhard's advice, and it is also part of the monastic tradition. In his Rule, Benedict is very critical of idleness. But *joie de vivre* plays an important part in it. At the end of the prologue to the Rule he writes, "The monk should not immediately be dismayed and run away in fear from the way of salvation, whose entrance must necessarily be narrow. But as we advance in monastic life and faith our heart will be enlarged and we will run in the way of the commandments with unspeakable sweetness of love."

When Benedict sets the monk on the path of virtue, he never expects perfection. This is a big difference because someone who puts himself under pressure to be perfect will never be satisfied. Perfectionism is the enemy of joy. People who put themselves under such pressure are tragic figures. They will never be content, they are always chasing something they can't achieve. They constantly fall short of their goal. Men who work frantically at achieving the perfect body through body-building, or young women who starve themselves to death because they want to look like the supermodel Heidi Klum, are tragic figures.

Benedict also sees that perfection carries with it the danger of pride. In his Rule he is trying to find a middle way "to meet the requirements of the strong and prevent the weak from running away." This is typically Benedictine.

The joy of a big heart transmits itself to others. I always find it with people who are successful in life. You can't wait until the end of life to find real joy. There are people who realize this very early on and others who learn this in the course of their lives. I always like to talk about a particular confrere who has in the meantime passed away, who was such a person. With his straightforwardness and his humour he was able to call everything into question. He was able just by making a small comment to bring everyone back to reality and nothing ever threw him off course. He could sit there and listen to all the arguments and bring them all down at the end like a house of cards with a single question. This is what I call sovereignty and a state of cheerful serenity.

This same monk sat opposite me in the choir of our monastery church. Sometimes I saw him smiling. When I asked afterwards, "What were you thinking about again today?" he only ever said, "It's just so beautiful." Usually it was something mean that had passed through his mind, which he commented on by saying, "It is better to annoy other people than be annoyed with yourself. It's healthier."

We can be good to ourselves and ought to be good to others. If I believe I am loved and accepted as I am, I do not have to desperately try and find myself in order to accept who I am. Many people whose parents did not give them enough attention look for themselves throughout their lives. A child who has grown up in normal circumstances doesn't have to find himself, he knows who he is. His mother, father, brothers and sisters have given him the necessary self-confidence. Of course later on we also need the kind of support that is very effective in a marriage, when, for example, the husband tells his wife how beautiful she looks and how much he enjoys her company. And when the wife says to her husband in a critical situation, "Don't be despondent, it's not the end of the world." This is the kindness and affection we should give each other because it does us good and is important for our mental health.

To find joy in life you have to take life as it is. Life is not infinite and human beings are not perfect. Humour is the appropriate attitude. In the words of Oscar Wilde, "Life is too important to be taken seriously." I smile at the little imperfections of life from a certain distance and do not like to condemn anyone who does not measure up to my standards. Basically everyone wants to be able to take such a relaxed view. Who wants to live permanently under pressure to be perfect?

"Be joyful and let the sparrows chirp", said Don Bosco. That is Christian serenity. I accept that the world is not infinite but limited. Then I can work things out, weigh everything up and act. A world in which we meet each other under these conditions looks very different from a world that has fallen into the hands of the perfectionists and moralists.

And consciously taking time for something which gives you pleasure, is something everyone can set out to do. This is how I try to live myself. Recently I gave a performance with my band together with the famous rock group "Deep Purple" in the monastery of Benediktbeuern. I take time for occasions such as this. Even though some people who do not know or understand this music think rock music is the music of the devil.

I am not bothered if strict pietists are against this. In Allgäu where I come from, a lot of people belong to the Reformed Church. As a small boy I frequently played with the children of a pharmacist, and felt very much at home when I went to their house. The children's magazine which I read there was however anything but entertaining and amusing. It seemed to be infused with a permanent air of mourning. Confronted with such a profound consciousness of sin I said to myself at the time, "I could never be a Protestant, it's all so sad." But then later on I met very humorous Protestants such as the theologian Karl Barth, who got up every morning with Mozart's music and hoped he would still be able to listen to Mozart in heaven.

For me rock music is also a sign and expression of *joie de vivre*. When the plane is landing I sing "On the Highway to Hell," a song recorded by an Australian hard rock band. And then, with the same pleasure, I sing Led Zeppelin's "Stairway to Heaven." Why should we take everything so deadly seriously? Can't we also look at such texts ironically?

We all are born for joy. And we should allow ourselves this joy. This applies to everyone, not only to the young rock fans who love and lose themselves in this music but to the whole population, young and old, including the monks in their monasteries.

Joy is the most effective deterrent against fear. If in my monastery the monks are one day discussing what they remember about the various abbots, what this one built and organized, what that one achieved, and then ask themselves what they remember about my time, I would be very happy if they said, "We were no longer afraid."

That would be the best compliment anyone could pay me.

2 The Big Question

THE big question is what should we do with our time, with our lives? What should be our priorities? One answer in the Rule of Benedict initially seems rather shocking: "All the time the monk should be aware of death."

It sounds like denial of life and asceticism but it is quite the opposite.

Benedict's injunction reminds me of a picture book by Wolf Erlbruch entitled "The big question." A child goes round asking people, animals and objects "the big question": "Why are you, and why am I in this world?" He gets very different answers. His brother, for example, says, "You were born to celebrate birthdays"; his grandmother, "You are in the world so that I can spoil you, of course." The bird says, "You are here to sing your song." He even asks the stone, which says, "You are here in order to be here."

Finally the child asks death as well, who answers, "You are here to love life."

How can they be related: knowledge of death and love of life?

David Steindl-Rast, a Benedictine brother who is now

over 80 years old, once described why he felt called. He grew up during the war in Austria and one of his fundamental experiences was of death. His young friends were called up and died, "But in spite of this," he said, "being reminded of death every day, my youth was the most brilliant and beautiful you can imagine. In spite of all the terrible things. It was full of unquenchable vitality. And then the war was suddenly over. And I was alive. I was 19 and never thought I would live to be 20. Quite by chance, if chance really exists, I had read the Rule of St Benedict, which was forbidden literature at that time. There it said that the monk should always be aware of death. And suddenly I realized that we were so happy because we were always being confronted with death. That was why we had a completely different relationship to time and to life."

It is not just extreme situations like war that force us to realize that our time is limited. It can be the experience of illness. The death of somebody the same age or of a young person. Or an accident we have narrowly escaped. I have had many such experiences in my own life. They give time, our lifespan, an entirely new quality. We live more intensively, consciously and attentively.

"The unpredictable death daily in your mind" is thus a piece of advice given by Benedict not to make us afraid but to enable us to properly assess the values of this world. This sentence comes in the chapter about the spiritual instruments or spiritual exercises. What this tells us is that we can acquire this attitude, which protects us from false alternatives, simply by practising it. Every day. By remembering our finiteness we can recognize what is really important and enduring in our lives. Awareness of this kind teaches us detachment, so that we don't get too involved in superficial and unimportant matters.

It is not death that makes us unhappy. We become unhappy if we suppress it and behave as if we could escape it. When we feel how fleeting time is, we must not panic and try to flee ourselves. I often find that people who cannot accept death live as if they were trying to pack two or three lives into one. A lot of the rushing around in our lives is perhaps also due to this. Hunger for experience out of fear of not getting enough out of life.

It says in the Bible: "Only wisdom knows the end of time." A call for serenity. That is by no means easy.

Opposite our house in my home town was a butcher's shop. The lady who ran it had five sons, four of whom were killed in the war. The last son was going to take over the shop. One day, when riding his motor bike to Munich, he missed a red light and had a fatal accident. It is impossible to imagine what could have been worse for his mother. In addition, she was diabetic and had to have one leg amputated. The butcher's shop finally went to a distant relative.

This woman lost everything of value to her, everything that had previously been her life. I always visited her during my holidays when I was at the St Ottilien seminary. I can still see her sitting in front of me in her wheelchair, at peace, with her rosary in her hands. However, she was anything but a religious bigot. We talked to each other a lot and she said to me, "You know, I have no idea what all this is good for. I can't fathom it. But I do know that our fate is in God's hands and so I pray and in my thoughts I am with God. I know one day it will all be over and that this is still my life." She bore her situation but not with gloom and despair or resignation. For her death was release in the positive sense. She was exceptionally wise to say that everything is in God's hands. To give herself up to this and let everything else go. She who had been a very canny businesswoman who stood in her butcher's shop and said, "Can I give you a little more?" and whom we always watched to see if she would cut her finger. And suddenly everything had fallen away and everything that had been important before was secondary. Now she could accept things as they were without having to assess their value. She could accept things that were unimaginable for other people and that she herself would not previously have been able to imagine.

The knowledge that our life has an end can make us wise. Our lives are really timed by death, our lifespan is measured by this earthly limit, but our hopes go beyond this.

If somebody were to ask me to sum up how Christians see time, my answer would be that our understanding is that we are only guests in this world. As it says in the well-known hymn ". . . we are only guests in this world and wander without rest through various tribulations to our eternal home."

One of the most beautiful texts in medieval spiritual literature is ascribed to my patron Notker the Stammerer, who was a monk in St Gallen in the ninth century. Notker is said to have composed the antiphone "Media vita in morte sumus" after observing workers who were dangling above a precipice as they constructed a bridge. "In the midst of life we are surrounded by death." When I hear this text I am always reminded of the accident during the construction of the Brenner bridge. I travelled under this bridge by train twice during this time and marvelled at the people who were working at a giddy height, who then one day fell to their deaths.

The life of human beings is limited but it has a goal. Our time may be limited by death, but it is not determined by death. Our time, like our dying and our death, is in the hands of God. The advice in the Benedictine Rule that the monk should constantly be aware of death simply means don't fool yourself. Death is the destination of our earthly journey but not the end of life. Death is part of our nature. This is not a threat but a memento. Benedict does not want to make us afraid but is telling us not to have any illusions. Nothing in this world has eternal value. Use your time and don't waste it, one day it will be over. Don't hold on to anything earthly. Focus *now* on the things of true value.

Everything that happens here is limited. The longing for eternity will only finally be fulfilled in the glory of God, when our restless hearts will find peace in Him. But for Christians every moment in this world is important too. This is why Christianity rates time so positively. Our lifespan is precious, a gift. And it is precious because it is something we can lose. But time is also relative. It vanishes when we die. Christians know that unity with God will take them out of time and into God's eternity.

With the prospect of death, time takes on a new significance. It becomes relative and it becomes more important. If somebody tells me you must make meticulous use of your time every day because God will one day add it all up, I always say, "I think God has given me the time in this life for my pleasure as well." However much I do, however energetic I am, I will never earn heaven through my own efforts or work. That is why I can also look calmly at my life, since for me time does not have absolute value. It does not have this anyway, because it is fleeting and superseded by eternity. Only if I consider my transient and finite life to be something absolute will it become tragic.

Over the years I have become more and more conscious of the fact that life is a gift. It is not totally in my hands. I am happy for every day. I am happy for every year. I am happy about everything I can do. I can still take pleasure in quite simple things like having time or the possibility to have a conversation.

It is precisely because time is limited that it is so precious.

I have no problem at all with dying.

But everything is still so beautiful.

3 The Meaning and Limits of Work

IN the ancient world, someone who had to work was called a pariah. He was an outcast in a society of free people. Leisure was what distinguished the free people from the slaves. "Otium," the Latin word for leisure, means the time for the really important things such as philosophy, art and public affairs. "Negotium", business, negates this ideal. The thinkers of ancient times even assumed that working for a living was damaging to character. In Rome craftsmen were thus not allowed to take office in the government. Politicians, orators and lawyers didn't work, they were people of leisure. In Rome it was against the law to ask money for legal advice.

In the Bible, work is also "cultivating and preserving" (Gen 2:15). This is also in the psalms. And Psalm 65 praises the harvest: "The valleys deck themselves with grain, they shout and sing together for joy." But it is not only something pleasurable. Here we also find "By the sweat of your face you shall eat your bread." While according to this work is seen as a divine task, it is also associated with sin. And with the idea of burdens and drudgery. "The years of our life are seventy, or ever by reason of strength eighty; yet their span is but toil and trouble; they are soon gone, and we fly away" (Psalm 90:10).

While leisure was clearly valued very highly by the Greeks and Romans, a new attitude became evident with St Benedict. In Roman times nobody would have used the same word for political activity, work in the fields and housework, but Benedict said, "The monks should not be aggrieved when they have to do their own harvesting." He reasoned that "Only when we live by the work of our own hands like our fathers the apostles are we true monks."

The founder of western monasticism begins the chapter on work in his Rule with the sentence "The devil finds work for idle hands." In his opinion, idleness is the enemy of the soul. Otium becomes otiositas, leisure becomes idleness. And this is why he writes that the abbot should give monks manual work to do if they don't want to read, as it were for prophylactic reasons. Even the sick should be given light work so that they don't become idle and endanger their souls.

Freedom or subordination, burden or pleasure – work still has two sides to it. Today work is something you do to earn money and make a living. And, by contrast with the ancient world, it has increasingly become something which gives you freedom, creates independence and makes life meaningful.

But the two sides still remain, because today we constantly talk more of work in terms of a burden, in terms of the pressure that causes stress for so many people in modern industrialized societies, prevents them from finding the right balance between work and life and gives them no more time for what we call leisure, which is no longer synonymous with free time. Leisure is the time when I can be active in my own interests.

It was precisely a model for this work-life balance that Benedict was creating when he combined work and the monastic life, an active and a contemplative life. It was a new understanding of work and time, a new ethical approach to the world that the Benedictine monks brought to the west. Prayer and work, religious services and working in the fields are one. "Ora et labora" means that people are balanced when their everyday activities and their focus on eternity, in other words their relationship to the world and their relationship to God are combined. Both of these things are the purpose of our being: we invest our strength in our work and develop our powers, but we do not exhaust ourselves with work.

Benedict has added a third element to "Ora et labora," "lege"- read: read the Bible and the writings of the fathers of the church. He allots specific times for daily reading and Sunday is to be totally free for it. This was almost certainly not easy for small monasteries, when we remember that at that time you could not just go out and buy a printed book in a bookshop. Every book had to be copied out by hand. But this mental and spiritual nourishment was so important for Benedict that he allowed enough time for it: leisure became fulfilled time.

The German philosopher Immanuel Kant, whose

writings are basically still within the framework of the Christian tradition, said that "the more occupied we are, the more alive we feel." Work takes precedence as something that is valued positively.

Here it is clear that work is no longer a symbol of bondage. Work and structured leisure time belong together and are what characterizes human life.

Since working time has become more important as part of life and as a purpose of life, in our modern industrialized society this has given rise to questions of an entirely different kind.

Some people have little to do, and others have too much. The pressure is increasing and fewer and fewer people have more and more to do. Of course, by this I am not talking about those people who simply have to have a lot to do. As the saying goes: if you want something done, give it to a busy person.

Artistic activity is perhaps a special case. Even in the ancient world it was not looked on as drudgery. And when we think of an artist like Lüpertz who creates sculptures out of tree trunks, he probably doesn't find the moving and processing of these heavy pieces of wood drudgery. The people who had to fell the trees probably felt differently about it. And an artist like Serra, who welds large pieces of iron together, will see his work quite differently from the way a welder in a factory sees the same activity.

Aside from creative work, however, work is generally determined by someone else. You are involved in a process planned and determined by others. You have to do something others have ordered you to do or which is established as part of specific processes. Simply allowing yourself to be ridden over roughshod by others is however something completely different. The important thing is to bring your self-confidence and pleasure in creativity into the work situation.

People like to be productive, to express themselves in what they do, to make a contribution and to be active. You also feel that you are worth something through your work. And someone who does nothing is in great danger of becoming frustrated. André Gorz, the French social philosopher, was a proponent of the unconditional basic income. Later he distanced himself from this idea. He gave an interesting reason for changing his mind. He said that this logically supported the refusal to do *anything* at all.

That is the danger. And that is also the reason why I have problems with the idea of an unconditional basic income. It's the same as in the developing countries. Here people are made dependent through development aid and see no reason to take any initiative themselves. People who are given everything finally do nothing at all of their own accord. Why should they? It is tempting and convenient just to take the money. Why should they make any effort? When we promote such an attitude, we destroy the person, his freedom and his creativity. He gets used to being passive.

Work, seeing that I am needed and useful, also for others, is part of my life; I earn my living with what I do and when I am tired in the evening, because I have worked hard, then I know what I have done.

In the 1960s, there was a vocational crisis for many of the monks in the monasteries, primarily the priests. The lay monks or lay brothers who worked as carpenters, shoemakers or craftsmen could see in the evening what they had done with their day. For priests involved in pastoral care this is not usually so obvious.

A similar situation can arise when somebody reaches pensionable age or stops work. Anyone who is no longer involved in the work process is then in the position of not "having" to do anything and is not "needed" in the same way as in the past. But in this situation too you need goals to make life interesting. I myself need goals to motivate me. This being pushed, being driven in a positive way towards a goal makes sense. I would become idle, which was what Benedict criticized so much, if I had nothing to stimulate me.

But a stimulus of this kind does not have to come from work. There are many meaningful activities that are essential for our society.

In the ancient world, the concept of leisure included having time to get involved in social affairs and being active without receiving money or a salary for it. I think it is very good when people do voluntary work or are creative to the benefit of society. These people find meaning in life when they work from morning till night as they did in their jobs. People who take on responsibilities will also benefit personally from this. Recently I read about some older people who are acting as mediators at a school in a problem area. They help the children to talk to each other about their problems and conflicts instead of immediately using their fists. And someone told me about a grandma-grandpa project. Some parents have no time because they are working. And then there are immigrant parents who can't help their children with their school work for language reasons. Here the grandma-grandpa project steps in and provides the children with what they need. All those who are involved in such a project of course take on responsibilities and commit themselves. But this is what holds a society together, when people give their time to others without always expecting money. Wanting to be of use to others, promoting community life, this is meaningful.

In Germany there is a tendency to think equal opportunities are the answer, in education too. But what use is it if a child has no support from the family, and comes from a milieu where education is not valued or is even seen in a negative light? I know of such cases, where even today children are told, "Mind you don't get too clever. You don't have to read all the time." Supporting such children and helping them overcome lethargy and the indifference of their parents is an important task.

Equal opportunities must come from the base. Everybody must contribute. I myself grew up in the country and when I – together with others from our village – had to take the entrance exam for the Oberrealschule (at the time a mathematically oriented grammar

school) in Memmingen, all our teachers were aware that we did not have the same chance of passing as the children from the town. I had a teacher at the time who prepared eight of us for the exam for six weeks without payment. With his tutoring, two of us obtained the best marks in the exam. That was equality of opportunity and it was made possible because someone helped. The same background does not mean the same starting conditions for everyone. And this is still the case today. For this reason we need one another – and we need people who have time for others.

Usually these are people who are retired but want to do something constructive – also for their own benefit.

There are of course also people who after a hard working life say now I want to enjoy my time. They are right, although it is a pity if they couldn't enjoy themselves before. But once your career is over, there is still no need to twiddle your thumbs and be bored.

To be able to stop, let go and relax. This is the art of living, and shouldn't only apply after you retire. You must not only be able to stop when you are having an argument. You must also be able to stop when you are working and even when you are celebrating. However much we might long for things to last and want a happy moment to go on forever, we also have to recognize at some point that that was enough. It was very nice. But we've also got other things to do. The person who stops when things are at their best has the best memories of the activity or event in question and doesn't want more.

Being able to stop is not only an art, it is a decision. Even with work you have to know how to stop. Perfectionists never finish what they are doing. You must be able to say that's enough. I must leave it at that, I could perhaps improve on it, but it's good enough. Being able to stop also means accepting your own limitations.

You also have to be able – at some point – to give up your career. This means also saying goodbye to everything that may have been involved in terms of structure, power and privileges. This applies not only to the minister who suddenly no longer has a chauffeur, a cook and a secretary and to the boss for whom no-one holds the door open any more. When work was part of your life and identity and suddenly all this ceases, it can come as a shock. If my life is only defined in terms of work, I have to ask who am I when I don't have this any more.

Times of work and non-functional times of prayer are related to one another in the daily life of a monk. Every day throughout his life is organized in this way and it is these two elements in combination that give meaning to life. But the same applies to everyone. To do something meaningful, to work, to use your time, is important. But that is only one aspect. I was not born only to work. Leisure is part of our lives as well.

Sören Kierkegaard says, leisure is divine, so long as you are not bored. Leisure can of course lead to idleness if I just sit and doze. Dozing can be good now and then, but that is a form of relaxing. Relaxing means letting go of tension.

Tension and relaxation are related. There are areas where tension is inappropriate, times of creative rest: this is when you turn to others, cultivate relationships, have a meal or a conversation with someone. When you are not under strain but when something important is nevertheless taking place. And then there are times of high tension, which are equally creative: an artist or researcher forgets to eat because he is so involved in his creation or the problem he is trying to solve. He feels his stomach rumbling but what he is doing is more important. This is the real freedom of a human being. An animal would then stop.

Relaxation is human. And tension is human. The two are related. The message preached by certain devotees of wellness and relaxation is an obstacle to creativity. It is narcissistic self-centredness. And it is ultimately merely sleep-inducing and boring.

Muscles have to relax in order to be able to work again. Relaxation creates new tension and new strength.

4 Dropping out is not an Option

WE'RE not living on an island like Robinson Crusoe. We can't slow down the tempo of our world any more than we can change the speed at which our globe revolves around the sun.

We can adjust the tempo at which we operate according to the situation and needs of the moment. To want nothing to do with the tempo of the modern world would be to opt out of civilization. Besides, not even Robinson Crusoe, abandoned far from civilization on an island, could opt out of time. In Defoe's story, after only ten or twelve days on his island, Robinson is already longing for ways of measuring time. His greatest problem is that without paper, pens and ink he cannot calculate the passing of time and might "even forget the sabbath days from the working days." So he carves notches in a post, small ones and longer ones. In his words, "and thus I kept my calendar, or weekly, monthly and yearly reckoning of time." We always, therefore, live in a time frame. Ours today is much faster than Defoe in the nineteenth century could ever have imagined.

To opt out of the tempo of our world is a romantic idea, perhaps also a kind of utopia – like Plato's idea of the state. If Plato's idea of the state became reality it would not be a "critical idea" anymore, as it is in the understanding of the author.

Criticism of the hectic pace of our world is of course justified. But it is not in our power to stop the world and suddenly make everything go more slowly. If I lived at the pace advocated by the hero in Sten Nadolny's novel "The discovery of slowness", not only the economy would not function, neither would anything else. Then in the end the author wouldn't even have the money to write a book about discovering slowness.

But I also wouldn't go so far as to say that the constant increase in tempo is a law of nature. We come up against our natural limits. There is the often-cited story of the gazelles and the lions in Africa. Every morning in Africa when the gazelles wake up, they know that they have to run faster than the fastest lions, or they will be eaten. And every morning the lions in Africa wake up knowing that they must be faster than the slowest gazelles otherwise they will starve. Ultimately it's all the same whether you are a gazelle or a lion: when the sun rises, you've got to get up and run. Both of them will exert themselves, but within the limits imposed on them by nature.

We are not animals . . . but we can still learn for example from the Grimm's fairy-tale of the hare and the hedgehog – in which the fast hare repeatedly exhausts himself totally in 74 races and in the end falls down dead. It shows us how to tackle challenges intelligently.

Nevertheless, as human beings we are governed by

the laws of nature. The trouble is that we are in danger of forgetting this with the permanent acceleration that is currently a feature of our world. Nature has long ceased to govern our time with the rhythm of the seasons and the clear alternation of day and night. But there is an inner rhythm which is part of our nature and has universal connotations. The person who can connect up with this rhythm can find great inner peace. By following it, he will be better able to shape his own life: the times of growing, of development, of harvest and of rest correspond to the pattern of human life.

This inner rhythm which connects us with the laws of nature should not of course be interpreted rigidly. People in the nineteenth century did not live as long as we do today. Hygiene and medicine have developed in the meantime so that disease has been reduced and we have become healthier. Nevertheless we can say today that people cannot live for more than 120 years. There are limitations and the limitation of death is one we cannot evade.

At the time of Benedict, the whole of society lived according to the rhythm of nature and did not question it. People also gave this natural rhythm a sacred meaning. We only have to think of the cult revolving around the rhythm of the sun – people knew that on 21 June the sun would shine through the huge gate of Stonehenge. The primitive peoples saw the passing of time in terms of rhythm and marked it with something visible. The seasons created as the earth revolved around the sun were experienced in the same way each time, in other words there was a rhythm to life. Rhythm is something that has life in it. It was always seen as something creative. As a created, given cycle on the one hand and as a creative process on the other: in spring nature is once again creative. It rests as it were over the winter in order to build up new strength.

A romantic desire for a slow world which simply denies the existence of industrialized society is not the same thing as the elementary desire for this natural peace, this cosmic rhythm.

On the other hand, it is clear that industrialization simply no longer allows us to live according to our natural rhythm. We only need to look at the attempt made by German industry to abolish public holidays. If time is only money, in other words is seen in a purely economic light, then it no longer has different qualities, it no longer has rhythm. The industrialists argue that they are not abolishing rhythm, but want to work on Sundays and public holidays and are operating according to the rhythm of the machines in order to utilize their capacity, because switching machines off and on is too expensive. Machines however only operate according to a mechanical rhythm, which has nothing to do with natural rhythm.

Permanent utilization increases the profitability of the machines. Our printing press in St Ottilien does not run on Sundays. In the past we only had one shift, but now we have two. If we worked during the night we would have three shifts. This would be more cost-effective, but we still don't do this – because of the people. Other companies work through the night. I don't know what effect it has on health in the long term if we submit ourselves to the dictates of machines. We need time to regenerate, just as we do when suffering from jetlag.

Regeneration is the opposite of constant pressure. A new study has been carried out on doping at work. More and more "top performers" take drugs, legal ones such as Ritalin and illegal ones such as cocaine, in order to be faster, better and more successful. They ignore their own limits and are prepared to risk the possible long-term consequences of burnout and the breakdown of their health.

Industrialized society wants to opt out of rhythm, time and actually out of nature itself. It wants to create its own world. Accepting the world as a creation is not part of its credo. Creation implies respect, respecting what you have been given. Industrialized society operates according to the principle of profitability – this is its most important value.

However, if we can't opt out of industrialized society, what can we do?

I recently read a report about a Chinese philosophical school. The name of the school translates as "Take a little time for yourself." The report however explained that it had another meaning in Chinese, which was "take responsibility."

This as I see it also applies to our current situation. We need more time, which again is the prerequisite for

seeing where we should take responsibility and acting on this.

On the one hand we have to think about the meaning and purpose of everything, about where our society is going and what its values are.

And on the other hand we need people who can take responsibility and are in a position to put things right when society has gone in the wrong direction.

Industrialized society is profit-oriented and sees everything in terms of doability. Human beings are always tempted to apply their skills to the point of exhaustion. This has produced technical miracles, but when the moral basis is missing, it can also lead to incalculable problems.

What can save us?

I believe that our salvation is the fact that we are not just individuals but are also part of a community. We can't control ourselves of our own accord, but in a community we can all control each other. Not in the negative sense of watching and mistrusting one another, but in the sense of solidarity. We have to support each other.

On my own, susceptible and tempted to try everything out, the enticement of evil will be great. The drug scene, for example, is dangerous for people who have no-one to stand by them. Some people would be lost if they were alone in such an environment, but the young man with a girlfriend who tells him to stay away from drugs will perhaps heed her and not do as he otherwise might have done. The same applies to society. Responsibility is taking the time to pause, observe what is going on and observe yourself, distance yourself, listen to others and talk about developments with them.

Reflection costs time and time is money. But to take this time will possibly also save a lot of money. We can't get around the economic aspect. Recently there were reports about how many billions the ecological catastrophe is still going to cost us and how expensive it will be to rectify the damage done by thoughtlessly carrying on producing. This means that it also makes economic sense to take time for reflection.

With the worldwide financial crises as a consequence of the speculation with virtual products, it has finally become clear that only humane, value-oriented economic dealings will be successful in the future. The time I take for reflection and checking is not wasted. I don't only minimize the risks, I also even save, because I avoid expensive redundancy. For example, someone testing pharmaceutical drugs will perhaps take ten samples, but to get results that are really accurate requires a hundred samples. The more time that is taken for more precise examinations and reflection, the more mistakes can be avoided. The cost-benefit calculation is however also part of the equation.

Diderot says, "If you've gone the wrong way, you will get more lost the faster you go."

And there is also a proverb that says, "What is the use of running if you're not on the right path?"

5 The Tempo of Life

SOMEONE has calculated how long the average person in Germany is on the move, in trains, metros or cars. Someone of 70 will have spent more than four years en route. With me it would probably be much more.

I often get asked how I can reconcile such a life with the Benedictine *stabilitas loci*. Stabilitas however doesn't mean immobility but an anchorage from which, in the course of time, inner stability grows. This inner grounding is what matters.

Flexibility is not in itself something negative. But I can only be flexible from a fixed point since I will otherwise lose my bearings. Even the most flexible employee needs time and a fixed place for withdrawal. For me, being part of a community and an established rhythm stabilizes me in the midst of my hectic professional life.

The body needs its phases of relaxation, for good biological reasons. Usually it takes some time after a stressful period for the body as well as the mind to calm down.

Even when we are assailed with demands from every direction, there is one way of deflecting these claims on us: *presence.*

On my flights around the world I sometimes experience summer before winter or suddenly spring comes in between the two. When I fly to South Africa I enter another climatic zone and go from summer to winter. Or I sometimes land in autumn from spring. There have been years when I had no spring at all. I particularly missed blossom-time in May in St Ottilien, where we have beautiful apple trees that are in full flower at this time of year. Sometimes the blossom was not yet out when I went away and was already over when I returned. Of course then I do miss something and of course the time differences are also disturbing. But I easily adjust. It is as if I were just going into another room. I hardly feel that I am in a different time zone. I am now simply "at home" wherever I happen to be. I do not feel the time differences, by contrast with many people who in a similar situation find it difficult to acclimatize and take a long time to do so. I arrive and am at home. *I am there* – and plunge into my work as if I had never been anywhere else. And the upheavals are not so bad at all because they succeed one another so quickly. I have no time to experience them as upheavals. And this also has to do with presence: with arriving somewhere and immediately being *there* – as in Zen meditation.

To remain balanced, you must frequently drop your anchor. My anchor is being in my own four walls now and again. It does me good every so often to sleep in my own bed and sit at my own desk and attend to a few essential matters. When I have been at home for a short while, then I am able to set out again. When I am away

I try to be fully present for the people I meet. I am there. I am open for these people, and enjoy their pleasure when they show me everything. And even if it is also a bit hectic when they are taking me around it is still also delightful. People's love can be almost overwhelming. But it is also a support and an anchor.

Of course I take the European concept of time with me when I travel. The Africans, for example, do not live at a fast pace. There is an African proverb which says that when God created the world he gave the Europeans clocks and them time. This expresses their mentality: if I don't come today, I'll come tomorrow. I belong to a culture to which God gave clocks and when I meet people to whom he gave not clocks but time then I am usually the one who is saying, "Let's get a move on!"

You can't get away from your own conception of time. When I was Archabbot of St Ottilien I flew to Africa two or three times a year and I simply allowed more time for these trips. I make up to two weeks free for my visits to Africa, so that no other appointments can get in the way. In other words, I adapt myself to the others and in this respect I am fully *there*. In such situations I am also not constantly looking at my watch since this would drive me crazy and make the others nervous.

It is clear that the tempo of the world and our lives is constantly getting faster. Nobody can get away from this. But the most important thing is to know who I am and what I want. It is not a question of choosing between the alternatives of slow or fast. I must know what is required when. A runner must run if he wants to win. But you can't keep on running. The person who is always complaining about the tempo of the world should ask himself who is pushing me if it is not I myself? Or could it be that I allow others to push me? It can then be a great help to set oneself priorities.

An Asian proverb says that if you want to reach your goal quickly, you must sometimes make a detour. Tempo is relative. You must not always go the fastest way, the important thing is go the right way.

The general favouring of slowness over swiftness is romantic. There are things that simply have to be done quickly. Lightning does not descend slowly from heaven, it flashes down, because that's its very nature.

Tempo originally only meant pace and not quickness. When we ask somebody what speed he's driving at, this has nothing to do with driving too fast. When I read over and again that speed merchants will be subject to severer punishments, what does that mean? Not only that traffic regulations are taking over the role of a punishing god, but that someone who drives at 53 instead of 50 is suddenly a speed merchant!

Tempo actually only means time, not speed. There are fast and slow tempi. And here too, it is not in people's nature to be the same at all times. At the age of 68 one cannot run as fast as a 16-year-old. But there are perhaps other advantages. And there are simply situations where hurrying is unavoidable. If I want to catch a train I may sometimes have to run. And if I've got behind with a piece of work, then at the end I have to catch up again and if necessary speed up.

What is considered "fast" and what "slow" has always changed from one age to the next. Mozart, for example, was played faster or slower in different epochs, according to the conception of time. The composer Beethoven took 60 minutes for his Eroica, when he conducted the premiere in 1804. The conductor Leonard Bernstein reduced the playing time at a later date in Vienna to 53 minutes and 20 seconds and was four minutes faster when he subsequently conducted it in New York. In 1987 Michael Gielen took only 43 minutes. We could of course say to this, haven't we even got an hour to spare?

But a new interpreter is a new creator, a new artist with a new concept of tempo. In this context there's no such thing as objectivity. Just as in life in general.

Everything has its time. Everything has its tempo. Our own lives are no different in this respect. The same approach is not always required. We should be able to play the music of our lives at different tempi. And as in music, there is a wide range of options for our lives: andante, presto, allegro. There are times of serene repose and relaxation. And there are prestissimo times.

Being fast is not everything. The example of the hare and the hedgehog shows that it is not always the faster one that wins, but the one that makes proper use of his abilities. When I am writing something, I notice that I can't work endlessly on a text. It is important to stop. Once I have a little distance, I look at the text differently and change it accordingly. Our brains need this distance in order to be creative, and this is the case with so many things in our lives.

Nor is slowness the answer. Some time ago I read a well-meant prayer. At the Catholic Conference in Osnabrück it was even printed in the official booklet. A romanticized glorification of tarrying and slowness. "Let me go slower, oh Lord. Steady my hasty steps. Release the tension of my nerves and muscles through the soft music of the singing water. Let me go slower to see a flower, to exchange some words with a friend, to pet a dog, to read a few lines in a book."

As well-meant as it was, and as idyllic as the situations are which this poetic and meditative text conjures up, my spontaneous reaction was: "No, Lord, let me nothing. This is not my experience."

My experience can be illustrated as follows: when I am travelling with someone else, and we have to hurry, for example when we are changing trains, it is still not an unpleasant experience because there are two of us. Because then I forget the time and don't suffer from being under pressure. My personal prayer would be the following:

"Lord, let me be open for everyone I meet.

Walk or run with me and let me forget the time

while we are together."

And when I do have to hurry and time is of the essence – God should run with me. When He is with me I will forget the time and its pressure will not affect me.

6 Taking off the Pressure

STRESS is not always something imposed from outside. We put ourselves under far too much pressure. After the death of my father I visited my mother as often as possible. I usually only had a short time with her. I had to take time for such visits out of a full timetable. But it was important for me to be with her even if it could never be for very long. And for my mother this time was precious and important as well. She was happy when I was finally back home again. She overdid herself with preparations and cooked an elaborate meal. And she was a very good cook. However, my time was also measured by the clock. Then I would keep saying, "Mum, please come to the table, I want to *talk* to you."

Taking off the pressure – I repeatedly tried to explain to her how good that would do her and me. I said, "I've been here for an hour and the whole time you've been in the kitchen, and afterwards you'll complain that I was only here for such a short time again." The way to a man's heart is not only through his stomach. Love needs time – time for each other.

Relaxing the pressure – that does not only apply to children. We need to have a different experience of time. Qohelet's saying "Everything in our life has its own time" is also valid for everyday life. There are times of pressure when we have to see that we get everything done and must finish all our preparations on time. And there are times when we have to do the washing-up, which is unavoidable if the crockery is not to stay dirty. But then we must stop, then we must have time again for something else. And beforehand we must have time to enjoy the meal or simply be with other people and enjoy the time with them. Adults as well need time to put their feet up and just stare into space. It is especially important for people under stress. It is the only way I can find myself again and when I do, I get fresh inspiration.

Recently during a visit to Munich I stayed on another evening to play the flute, to have two hours practice with a flautist for a concert. Afterwards she said, "You are staying for lunch, aren't you? What would you like? Something Bavarian? Sauerbraten or lights of veal?" A whole list of suggestions followed. I was delighted, and also astonished. Life does not just consist of planning and doing everything for a purpose. We men especially always need to be reminded that there are values that are at least equally important. There must also be time for these. And if I had not then said yes, the pleasure in our joint music making would have been halved. I am then also able to enjoy such a time and completely switch off from all the things that are pressing on me and waiting to be done.

Everything has its own time. It is not only a question of quickness or slowness, but also a question of taking off the pressure, also the pressure of time. It is removing time from its association with benefit and expediency. Just being there can be enough.

Certain things by their very nature just cannot be done under pressure and especially not under time pressure.

Try to "quickly meditate" – what an absurd idea.

Or can you drink wine quickly? No. What a terrible thought. Wine has to be drunk slowly, it has to be savoured, to dissolve on the palate, so that every nuance of flavour can be perceived if you want to enjoy it. Only an alcoholic can drink wine quickly, but he is then also drowning all his perceptive faculties.

It is the same with reading: if you are really immersed in a book, you don't want to reach the end quickly, but you are absorbed in the text and in another world, so that time no longer plays a part. Of course there are two ways of reading: one is flipping quickly through a factual text to get a rough idea of the content. The other is immersing yourself in a work of literature with its artistically complex language. There is nothing better than to be absorbed in a text and to enjoy or meditate on the form and beauty of a poem. I can't glance through a poem. I must perceive and savour every single word. Only then will I appreciate the beauty of a lyrical text.

And then there is the reading of the Bible, the "lectio divina", which is not the same thing as reading a spiritual text. Lectio divina means "ruminatio", ruminating on a text, which is how the monks described it in the past. And this is a quite different kind of reading. When I chant the psalms I know exactly what is in them, but I want to go even deeper into the text and repeat the words which have gripped me. Somebody has compared the psalms with the tides in the sea. Listening for the eternal breath of God which never ceases while reading these ancient writings is a way of getting involved in a text which is quite different from just consulting it to obtain information. Then all the reader does is open a door for a moment and close it again immediately. The reader who is absorbed in a text as is intended with the "lectio divina" is not just opening a door, he is entering another room. His soul expands and participates in the life, the breath of the spirit to which he gives himself up.

The person under pressure wants to reach a concrete goal, is propelled in a particular direction. He is not in the present. It is not possible to hurriedly pay attention to someone else. A person cannot be quickly caressed. Any woman would be horrified by the absurd idea of a quick caress. Tenderness and care are something people give to each other as a gift.

And this needs time and tranquillity. Only someone who radiates such tranquillity does others good.

When somebody comes into my room to talk to me and sees me smoking a pipe, this immediately creates a different atmosphere. The person knows this man has time. For me, a pipe is not the same thing as a cigarette. Instead of addictively pulling at a cigarette like some smokers do, pipe smokers are on a different temporal plane. They observe the smoke and are altogether more relaxed. There is something congenial about the whole process. And this too is a time factor. It's a form of self-defence against pressure. But I don't want to sound like an advertisement for pipe smoking. Other people will acquire other methods or weaknesses.

The only thing that helps against pressure is to deliberately take your time. Defend yourself against being totally pressurized.

> Let us treat ourselves to breaks. Let us allow ourselves rests in the midst of activity.
>
> Once again: Everything has its own time. . . .

7 Relaxation Gives us Strength

WHEN I was teaching philosophy in Rome in the 1970s, I met a group of young musicians, the "Nuova Consonanza", who performed their works every week in various halls or cellar localities. Afterwards we would sit together over a meal and talk until late in the night.

These musicians were fascinated by the free tempo and expression of the Gregorian chants. They came to mass in Sant'Anselmo every Sunday. I was the choir master at that time and interpreted the chants from the medieval neumes and rhythms, which leave a lot to the performer and are determined by the text. This and of course the religious intensity of the monastic liturgy greatly impressed these young artists.

At this time I also got to know the music of John Cage. John Cage was a musician inspired by Zen Buddhism, a legendary composer and key representative of avant-garde music. One of his famous compositions for piano is called "4'33." The premiere in 1952 was a scandal. The composition consists of 4 minutes and 33 seconds when nothing is played. A pianist comes onto the stage, sits down and does nothing. There is only silence. This composition, which is almost more like a happening, expresses criticism of a society that is constantly noisy, a society in which something always has to be going on.

Many people do not experience the different times of day when they power through it non-stop without taking a break, except perhaps 20 minutes for lunch, and then go home in the evening completely exhausted and just collapse. Everything has its own time, and the different qualities of time must be perceived and experienced. We can't act as if they were all the same.

Breaks are constructive. They are part of life and revive you because they provide release from concentrated activity and allow you to breathe. Structuring the day with breaks is something manual workers know how to do. In Baden and in Switzerland the first break, "z'nüne", is at 9 o'clock in the morning. In Bavaria this is called "Brotzeit", literally time for bread. This incidentally corresponds to the "Terce" in the monks' liturgy of the hours. This is the hour when we take a break. And in the afternoon at 4 o'clock there is another break, "z'viere", which is the equivalent of the tenth hour of the monastic liturgy. I have always envied our craftsmen and agricultural staff because they are able to take a healthy break and thus remain efficient. People working at a desk think they can keep going continuously throughout the morning. Even in a big company the wage and salary earners are often better off, because the unions make sure there are official breaks.

There is the fast tempo, the slow tempo and the break. A break cannot be seen in terms of an absence of speed.

When we take a break it is not a question of reducing our tempo, of just going slowly. A break is a constructive link – a free space – between the various tempi and activities. It is not nothing or doing nothing, it is something separate, but it is still part of the rhythm of life.

When we take a break we sharpen our perceptions, see more clearly and hear better. The best example of this is children who drop back when out walking with their parents. The children have discovered something along the path – ants or beetles – which their parents haven't noticed because they are walking too fast. When things flash past me too quickly, I don't see them at all.

Breaks provide structure and organize time. In music this is very clear: a pause does not indicate "stop playing". A pause gives structure and a form to a composition. Of course music has its beat. I am still fascinated by the free rhythm of the Gregorian chants. In freer forms of music there are also pauses. There is a rising cadence ("Aufgesang") and a falling cadence ("Abgesang"). In jazz, for example, where musicians improvise the most, there are nevertheless absolutely clear structures. It is incredible. These musicians know all the modes of a single key. They play their eight modes and also the different rhythm groups. Only when musicians have mastered these can they play in a jam session. It is only then that the call and response pattern functions, a melody develops and is accompanied by the right chord sequence. Outsiders sometimes think it is chaotic. But those who have some understanding of it know that in spite of the inspiration, everything down to the smallest detail is structured: one musician plays the theme, the soloists take it up in turn and at the end they all play the theme together.

Freedom requires structure. And that is what makes life today stressful. We live very freely and no longer have any structure. Breaks are however part of our natural structure.

In music, pauses are a connecting as well as a creative element. They are more than a brief absence of sound, they have a positive purpose. A musical pause of half a bar or a whole bar allows the music to breathe.

In life, in the course of a day, it is no different. It is not for nothing that we speak of a creative pause. If we interrupt our activities, if we come to a stop, breathe, recover, and enjoy the time available to us without having to use it for any particular purpose, then we will once again gather new strength for our activities.

Even breathing, incidentally, is not continuous. There is a brief pause between breathing out and breathing in. Breathing is a law of nature. Breaks are also a natural element of our time structure. Ignoring this will have consequences.

It cannot be emphasized enough that there are physical and mental laws, and we could also say human laws. They are like laws of nature but their effect is more subtle. We can perhaps pretend they do not exist. But if you play with fire, you get your fingers burned and this also applies to the way we continuously exert ourselves. The fact that we need breaks is one of these laws. When we do without breaks, when we no longer have a normal rhythm, sooner or later the situation will be critical – or the body will take its own breaks by means of unconcentrated dawdling.

I always notice after a long-distance flight how my whole body is in a state of confusion, how sensitive I am, how irritable, to the point of jumpiness. It is not however helpful to do nothing. What helps me is meditating, playing music or immersing myself in the daily rhythm of the community.

Of course as human beings we are not strictly limited and we can occasionally work against nature to increase our possibilities. Now and then we can perhaps work through the night. But we will eventually collapse if we do it too often. We can also fast, but only for a certain length of time. We cannot get around the fundamental aspects of our lives. If we want to survive as human beings we must first accept that we are creatures of God.

The issue of the break shows this clearly: when there is no longer any physical or biological stability, we become frailer. Sometimes the body then claims its rights – and compels us through illness to take a break.

This is called a "forced break". Such forced breaks can even be useful and sensible. We are forced to recognize that we cannot permanently burden our body and our mind, because that does us no good. Only rest gives us strength.

As it says in the Bible: "Better one hand full of repose than two hands full of achievement to chase after the wind" (Ecclesiastes 4:6).

8 Every Moment is Sacred

MONKS start their day very early. Usually between 5 and 6 o'clock. Members of strictly contemplative orders get up even earlier and sing Vigils in the middle of the night. Of course a "normal human being" cannot live like this, and cannot, like the members of some contemplative orders, go to bed at 7 o'clock or half-past seven.

But many people who today go and stay in a monastery for a limited period of time to live with the monks, find that the structure and rhythm of the day is very beneficial.

In the sixth century, Benedict structured the monks' day very clearly with his Rule and gave every hour a special meaning.

There are seven canonical hours and the Office of Vigils. Seven times a day the monks should interrupt their work for the Divine Office – in accordance with the Old Testament psalm: "Seven times a day I praise you."

To live the day as we monks do is to experience it in its natural, God-given form. Every hour has its own particular quality. The different "hours", in Latin *horae*, do not divide up time like a clock, but signify the healing quality of the time we are living through. This is also why the Divine Office is called the liturgy of the hours.

A daily rhythm determined by regulated times of prayer still forms the basis of monastic life today. This regulated schedule is based on a particular idea of the quality of time. According to this, time is more then just a series of appointments and obligations, it is something different from the hourglass that symbolizes the running out of our lives. It is a creation and a gift. This idea of time is based on acceptance of the creation. Accepting the creation means experiencing and affirming what is given by God.

People's everyday lives were determined for much of history by the natural rhythm of time. Today we are more likely to say, "Everything has its own time, but I have no time." The rhythm of prayer and work, Sunday and working days, rest and exertion is out of balance. With their daily routine, the monks also remind us of the wisdom of the Bible: "Everything has its own time." They also remind us that everything is under God's blessing.

The so-called little hours, which should be a short break from work – from the third hour, Terce, (around 9 o'clock), and the sixth hour, Sixt, (around 12 noon), to the ninth hour, None (around 3 o'clock) – are combined in the Divine Office of many orders today to form a single daily hour. The Prime was abolished by the Second Vatican Council.

The morning hour or Matins – these are the hymns of Vigils (the night watch) and Lauds (the morning prayer)

– refers to the night or the breaking dawn. We hope, we keep watch, and we await the day. Lauds celebrates the dawn, the awakening of nature and the resurrection of Jesus which overcomes the darkness of death.

Terce celebrates the high point of the morning when the monks stop their work to pray for the succour of the Holy Spirit.

Sixt is the midday break. This is the hottest time of the day. In the midday hour, reference is made to the sun with a prayer that our spirit may not become too heated, and that all conflict be taken from us. "In your presence, powerful God, is coolness, peace and patience."

In the evening the work of the day is as it were accomplished. In the evening hour, Vespers, we ask God to shine in our hearts during the darkness of the night.

At the end of the official day we prepare for the night with Compline and pray to God for His protection.

With these hymns the whole person is integrated with nature and with the salvation history (salvation through the reading and understanding of scripture).

Of course today not all monks get up in the middle of the night. Even in the past this was not the usual practice. Getting up very early and having little sleep was by no means widespread as an ideal for monastic life. The question is whether it is typically monastic at all: in winter the monks slept until all hours. Even though Benedict only scheduled seven hours for sleep, in winter it was around nine hours. The Romans had no standard measurement of time. The hours at night in December corresponded to 75 minutes of our present time, while in summer they were only 45 minutes long, so that the monks then only got five hours' sleep. They went to bed when it got dark and got up at what we would find a very early hour. This however gave them a consistent seasonal pattern. With their *horae,* the monks' day was divided into twelve hours, from sunrise to sunset. This was of course adjusted according to the season, so that in winter the monks slept for up to nine hours and in summer only five, also working much more then.

The structure of the day in monastic life from Lauds to Compline is balanced – and not only with respect to prayer and work. There should be time not only for the *lectio divina*, but also for a siesta. Benedict says of the siesta that if monks want to chant psalms during the midday break, in other words the siesta, then they should do it quietly so as not to disturb those who want to sleep. Here the word love, which many invest with so much pathos, is simply understood as consideration for and sensitivity to others.

The schedule of the monks has another, quite different quality: it enables them to become open and perceive certain things for the first time. Benedict has given form to the day. The idea of ordering natural time ranked very highly with him and he structured the day in detail. But he was no casuist. He was interested in the matter in hand, not in edicts. Codification did not come until much later. Another example from the Rule of Benedict, concerning the drinking of wine, shows that he was not interested in making rigid decrees: "Even though we read that wine is by no means a drink for monks; yet since the monks of our day cannot be persuaded of this, we must at least agree to drink not to satiety but sparingly . . . We believe that a "hemina" (which ranges according to interpretation from a quarter to half a litre) of wine a day is sufficient for each. But those to whom God gives the strength to abstain should know that they receive a special reward. If the local necessities, or the work, or the heat of summer require a greater measure, it must be for the Superior to decide in the matter, taking care always that neither excess nor drunkenness overtakes them. But if the local conditions are such that not even the measure prescribed above can be supplied, but much less or nothing at all, let those who live there bless God and not murmur . . ."

This is why even today there are still no iron rules for the structuring of a day in a monastery. Today not only the hours have been adapted to the requirements of our time. Even the time of the Eucharist varies, and there are communities which also celebrate it in the evening. Saint John's Abbey in Collegeville however celebrates it at lunchtime and many students from the university take part. There are many reasons for structuring the day in different ways.

At our monastery in St Ottilien, the monks work in a great variety of areas, and must thus start at the same time as the employees from outside, in other words at half past seven. And working back, that means getting up at four-fifty. It becomes difficult when different schedules clash. It was always a major dilemma in St Ottilien. We have our farmers, who go out to the fields very early, and we have our bakers. We have early mass at 5 o'clock. And then there are the others: the craftsmen all start at seven thirty and school begins at 8 o'clock. It is not easy to accommodate everyone. Eventually a fixed rhythm will be established. But initially it may be necessary to juggle with various options and make compromises.

However it is regulated in individual cases, the important thing is that the daily rhythm of the monks is always integrated into the two dimensions of the time of grace of the salvation history and the natural time of the day. What is important is the feeling for the special quality of the time of every day, however ordinary it might be. Time is experienced consciously and sanctified through the Divine Office. In every hour we are reminded that time is not ultimately at our command but belongs to God and He gives it to us.

Every moment is sacred.

This governs all we do.

9 The Monks' Concept of Time

WHEN the Testaccio district in Rome, which lies below our monastery of Sant'Anselmo, wakes up in the morning, when cars are started, motorcycles roar into life and people go noisily to work or school, we monks are in church. I always think about the people outside and think that it is my calling and my good fortune to be in their midst.

When I am asked, "Where do you get your energy from?" my answer is, "It is the joy of being with other people. But it is also above all the Divine Office, the praying and singing in the monks' choir in church." The Divine Office is the time where I can simply let go. But this is not a state of emptiness but one of fullness. If I had to compare it with something I would say that it is an experience with all the force of a cascading fountain in summer.

Our day has a fixed structure. This rhythm makes me aware that I am privileged to be able to keep a great deal of time free for prayers.

When I am standing in the statio, the passageway to the choir at the front of the church where we monks assemble before the service, I leave everything which has been occupying me behind, even my biggest worries. It can all wait for half an hour. Now only God and concentrating on God is important. Then I suddenly realize that it is not only His time, it is my time too. The time for God becomes a gift to me.

The monks' time is dominated from early morning to the night-time prayer by the psalms. Psalms are poems and are part of world literature. They are both personal prayers and the prayers of a community. When Psalm 139 comes up – "For you formed my inward parts; you knitted me together in my mother's womb" – I know and experience deeply what it is about.

I stand there and sing, but I see the complete psalm in front of me in the way I perceive the whole text of a poem. A particular mood envelopes me. One could call it meditation or contemplation. I no longer look at every single word. Suddenly I simply feel a great freedom. These are words that for more than 3,000 years have repeatedly helped people to verbalize their experience and that is what I still feel today: praying as one of this endless stream of worshippers is incredibly liberating.

Society in the past had strict rhythms: the working year was broken up by holidays, which reminded people of another story – of the great events of the story of salvation. Many of these holidays no longer exist, while others have lost their importance, like Lent which is the time of preparation for Easter, or the Christmas period with the particular atmosphere of Advent. There was a fixed daily rhythm, with fixed customs and prayers.

In my childhood the rule was still "when the bell is rung for prayers, it is time for children to go home." And many adults still remember getting up with the sun and going to bed at sunset in their childhood. Children for whom the morning began with the singing of a song, and the evening with another sung by their mothers, had a wonderful experience: they understood that now it is day and now it is night. They knew that life had a fixed rhythm. These fixed points have become rarer, if they even exist at all.

The Muslims still have their Muezzin, which announces such "holy times" and reminds the people that it is the hour of prayer. And the monasteries still have this fixed rhythm. Other people must find their own structures. Perhaps this is why many people have become interested in monastery life again, because of its healthy balance.

Of course not everyone can structure their daily routine like the monks. But through the rhythm of the monks they are reminded of something important: today we have changed day into night and night into day. We romanticize nature but in reality we live a very unnatural life, which has nothing to do with the natural rhythms and puts us at risk of detachment from our real selves. We are bound to nature and remain so until our death and in death.

Even today there are many who dream of living with the sun as was common in my childhood, from sunrise to sunset, and see it as the epitome of a natural life. Those who lived like this could say at the end of the day, "Now the day has passed, now we can go leisurely to bed." When after a hard working day which lasts into the night we only get four or five hours' sleep, going to bed itself is not a pleasure, we fall into bed exhausted.

Repetition, concentration, orientation – these are the elements which characterize the daily routine of a monastery.

Repetition doesn't mean superficiality. This is one view, and it is not correct. It is only when people are superficial themselves that everything becomes superficial. People who work in offices have photos of their families on their desks. They look at them repeatedly with pleasure and can never look at them enough. And people newly in love will have a photo of their boyfriend or girlfriend in their wallet and look at it as often as possible. This is something very lovely.

Our day needs structure. I am often asked whether such structure would be possible in ordinary everyday life. Whether one could as it were find the monk in oneself in everyday life. My answer is basically yes, but it is difficult when such a structure is continually interrupted by one's job.

Everyone can give his day a form. It is actually essential. I am also familiar with this problem as a monk, because of my frequent travelling. When I fly around the globe, wherever I am, first thing in the morning I have to decide what I am going to do during the day. And in the evening I see that not everything has gone according to plan. But whatever happens, early every day I take time to contemplate and pray. This is the only way to start the day well. Of course if I am in a monastery I take part in the organized prayers.

Actually everyone not living in a monastery should be able to set aside one or two special times a day. Nobody can tell me they can't. If a manager says this, he's not a good manager, as the planning of such oases is part of good time management. Not much is required. It is sufficient to withdraw briefly after getting up, before or after breakfast, in order not to just rush into the day but start it very consciously. It is enough to just remind ourselves that God will accompany us on this day too. Or in the evening take time to reflect briefly on the day.

Something else is included in my life – and this I would advise everyone to do: take around ten minutes to read the Bible, even if it's only a few sentences. Take a particular passage and work through it slowly. The object is not to get through it in a week, but to reach a deeper understanding and internalize what you have read. When I get up from my 20-minute siesta after lunch, reading the Bible has priority, and if I don't have time for this spiritual reading then I can be short with others. Especially when the phone calls come from Germany. They all come between two, two-thirty and three in the afternoon, a time when you can't call anyone in Rome. If somebody calls then and asks, "Did I disturb you?" I say honestly, "Yes you certainly did!" Often much to the surprise of the caller.

Every day needs rhythm, rituals, and also repetition – structured time.

This is what the prayer times provide. This conscious focusing on God at regulated intervals affects our lives, concentrates and deepens them. It is an experience that can always be repeated and always renews us.

Not only once in a blue moon, but every day. Everybody in their assigned place in life.

So when our city district wakes up and the growing noise from the street outside enters our church where we are holding our service, then I think how wonderfully our lives can complement each other. The people in our district cannot live like we do and we cannot live like them. But the message of St Benedict about structuring time has lost none of its significance.

10 The Heartbeat of Life

MANY years ago I was standing next to a friend of mine, a priest, when an older lady said to him, "Father, here's a German mark, please pray for me." On another occasion an even older lady said, "Father, don't take it to heart when I don't listen to your sermon, but otherwise I won't get through my prayers." It's funny, of course, but there's more to it than that.

What actually happens in the liturgy? Do the people who come to church on Sunday experience a structured, sacred time?

In the past, the liturgy was often understood in terms of the priest doing everything for the congregation. This was the impression I had when I first went to Rome in the 1960s. Hardly anyone came to church. Why should they, the priest was doing it all for them. At the time none of the ordinary people understood a word of the Latin mass. In Germany the faithful were occupied during mass with singing hymns or praying the rosary. The time passed faster but that was not the point of the exercise. This was why P. Anselm Schott, a Benedictine Father from Beuron, brought out the Latin mass book accompanied by a German translation, so that the faithful could follow what was going on at the altar.

Benedict emphasizes the all-important nature of the liturgy. It is not, as he sees it, a formal exercise, but the heartbeat of life. For me it is also primarily an experience, a profound experience in which I repeatedly immerse myself. It is the source of my strength in everyday life. Not simply a retreat from everyday life or something separate from it. For me it is like opening a window in time to enter into God's presence, which is eternity. At this moment I experience immersion in eternity and the possibility of taking a piece of eternity with me. Eternity in these terms is another word for happiness or bliss.

It is not only when you are having a genuine, profound conversation that you don't notice the time, it can also happen in church. I am always pleased when people tell me after the service, "That was so beautiful we didn't realize two hours had passed", when they otherwise complain about everything that lasts longer than half an hour.

I only can communicate enjoyment of life when I experience it myself. This is also the principle behind the liturgy. The Eucharist, whether in a small group or on a bigger scale, is always a festival for me. At special services in Africa, when small children perform sacred dances throughout, or when the nuns or other groups sing and dance during the service and enter the choir with a kind of processional dance, then the whole congregation is affected, sings and sways and physically expresses joy. In

Europe it is of course different, but here too it is a question of inner joy and enthusiasm.

When I celebrate the Eucharist myself, time disappears and I am fully there, or entirely absent. When in the Eucharist the words of Jesus at the Last Supper are spoken, then Christ is really present in the room and time ceases to exist for me. This is a mystical experience of unbelievable liberation. Everything opens up and I am taken out of the constricting flow of time into another reality.

There is a traditional saying that at the birth of Jesus and at His death time stopped. There are hymns which celebrate this. What it means is that here something important, something so great is happening that it as it were lifts us out of time. It is true ecstasy, removal from finiteness. Time no longer exists.

Can people today still experience this mystical dimension of the liturgy? Romano Guardini asked whether modern people were capable of taking part in church services. Do people in our individualistic society of singles still have access to it?

Karl Rahner said the future of Christianity belonged to the mystics, those who had *experienced* something. What had to be done was enable the liturgy to be experienced as a source of renewal, a breath of eternity which lifted people out of the constraints of finiteness. This is the exhilarating aspect of the liturgy, that I am removed from worries about the future and attachment to the past and the infinite obligations of daily life.

This doesn't of course mean the liturgy is something

that happens outside our time and has nothing to do with it. On the contrary, it gives order and meaning to time. It gives us strength to structure our time by pointing us to the dimension of a sacred time, a time of salvation. This is the importance of the liturgy, and not taking up one saint after another in the liturgical calendar.

When the liturgy is properly celebrated, a natural and holistic experience of time is possible. Our problem is that we are out of touch with natural time and its rhythms. The experience of time that we can have in the liturgy takes us back to the original dimension of human existence. The sacred is made real to all of us and brought into our lives, which are limited by the present. The liturgy thus takes us out of the fleeting moment into other realms of experience.

Sacred architecture is also evidence of this. The alignment of the main axis of churches with an east-west direction in accordance with the sun which rises in the east and sets in the west is an old principle. The worshipper looks to the east in the direction of the rising sun, to the natural place where the sun makes its entrance. Many churches incidentally do not have the altar but the door at their eastern end. In Ravenna, for example, the church doors were opened in the morning so that the sunlight flooded into the church. The rising of the sun symbolized the resurrection of the dead. Church architecture in the early days of Christianity combined theology with cosmic reality: with the day, with the sun. We ourselves experience the sun as an exhilarating element. Light does the body good, another world appears and the sun lightens our souls as well, lifts depression and fills us with joy in life. Since ancient times the sun has been a major symbol: Christ was the invincible sun that never sets, *sol invictus*. And celebrating this ancient feeling is exactly what the liturgy is about. Psalm 19:2.5-7 says: "The heavens declare the Glory of God and the sky above proclaims his handiwork. . . . In them he has set a tent for the sun, which comes out like a bridegroom leaving his chamber, and like a strong man, runs its course with joy. Its rising is from the end of the heavens, and its circuit to the end of them."

Liturgy is the experience of natural time and simultaneously of eternity. This does not however mean eternity in death. When I once asked the abbot of an Orthodox monastery on Mount Athos what particularly characterized Orthodoxy, he said "the community of the saints". People who lived more than a thousand years ago and who are remembered in the liturgy are present. And not only these saints, the whole community of the church is there, from the beginning till the present day. It is an immense mystery. Think what that means when we celebrate All Saints' Day, it means that there are thousands of millions for whom Christ died who are now in some mysterious way present. It is like entering heaven.

In Christianity God Himself intervenes in history by becoming man. The experience of time standing still doesn't mean the end of history. We feel anxious if everything stops. To acquire a qualitative feeling for eternity and the presence of the divine is however something quite different from experiencing an absence of change. It is an intense experience of fullness, rather than one of deathly silence. Such an experience does not mean just turning inwards. The time structured by the liturgy is a force which has an effect on history. Time is renewed and the new time too is again salvation.

This is not a question of playing off prayer against action, or the church service against global responsibility. Every prayer, every service motivates our actions, focuses us on the creation and on other people. To act correctly, we need the times when we look at things from the other perspective. We cannot always live in a hectic mode. The celebration of the liturgy is a sacred time. It enables us to contemplate. This is not running away from action, on the contrary, it prevents our actions from becoming even briefer and more superficial. The experience of community and a natural life will orient us with our small goals towards God.

The value of the liturgy, its beauty and its importance, is the common experience it gives us of the mystery of our lives. Every service shows us that there is a universal, cosmic dimension to our lives. It is our great fortune, and it is available to us all. This is what I wish for everyone: the experience of eternity in such a community. This is the only real happiness.

11 The Treasure of Sunday

MANY years ago I was in Agrigento on the south-west coast of Sicily. After I got my doctorate, my Abbot gave me permission to go on this journey that I had long dreamed of. I was standing in front of the famous Concordia temple, a magnificent piece of architecture from the fifth century BCE which is impressively sited in the middle of the countryside.

My thought was that it must not only have impressed the Greeks aesthetically, it must also have overwhelmed them with its massive dimensions and the beauty of its proportions. And this applies even more to the majestic temple of Segesta, with its ochre-coloured Doric pillars, which stands all alone in a valley near Palermo. To see it is to understand something of God's power.

But for me there was also something mysterious and inviolable about the building, something alien, precisely because of this impressiveness, this stillness. There was something that made me shiver and I thought that is not the Christian God.

Another example of this is in Jakarta. The Muslims have built a pompous mosque right opposite the new Gothic cathedral, a French filigree steel structure from the nineteenth century. The mosque must be nearly fifty times bigger and it is also covered with gold. The clear message of this architecture for the common people is look, our God, Allah, is the great and powerful God.

How do we Christians experience God? In no way do I connect such pomp and the experience of such overwhelming dimensions with the Christian God. A Christian experiences God's sovereignty when he reads in the Bible how Jesus stood before Pilate or was victorious over death on the cross. Perhaps the Christian experience is reflected most clearly in the importance we attach to Sunday.

We know above all that work is prohibited so that we can participate in the Sabbath rest of God. We also speak of the commandment which instructs us to go to church on Sunday. So we speak of prohibition and commandment. St Benedict, who lived in the sixth century and in a culture which considered work to be slavery, had a different understanding of Sunday. He was convinced that we have to work in order to live. But what he said in his Rule was that while on weekdays there should be a rhythm of prayer and work, Sunday should be free for the *lectio divina*. There is time for this reading during the week too, but not so much as on Sunday. However he adds, "On Sunday let all occupy themselves in reading, except those who have been appointed to various duties. But if anybody should be so negligent and lazy that he will not or cannot study or read, let him be given some work to do so that he will not be idle." Even on Sunday.

1. Community of the Priory in Kumily, India in 2008.

2. Ride on an elephant as a gift from the community in Kerala in 2008.

3. The Abbot Primate reading the Gospel
in the monastery of Makkiyad, India in 2009.

4. ISBF-meeting in Makkiyad in 2009.

"Love is the greatest happiness.
And being together with others the greatest gift in life."
– Notker Wolf

5. The Conventual Prior Fr. James of Vijayawada and students of the St Benedict School welcoming the Abbot Primate in 2007.

"Children need confidence in order to be able to master life."
– Notker Wolf

6. Notker Wolf with the members of a student wind orchestra in Vijayawada in 2007.

"Peace and harmony, faith and music are for Notker Wolf all one, they are all divine and he is confident that God loves music."

7. Notker Wolf playing flute for students in Vijayawada in 2005.

8. Notker Wolf with the Benedictine Sisters of St Lioba in Bangalore in 2005.

"Gratitude is for me the heart of Spirituality."
– Notker Wolf

9. ISBF-meeting in Vijayawada, India in 2007.

"Healthy spirituality does not lead to suppression, but to freedom and joy in life."

– Notker Wolf

10. ISBF-meeting in Kappadu, India in 2008.

"Monkhood really means being free for God – and the world."
– Notker Wolf

11. Charity concert on Austrian Television with his Rock Group "Feedback" in 2003.

12. Talk show on German Television with TV host Gottschalk in March 2007.

13 & 14 Visit to the bishop Jin Luxian of Shanghai, China in August 2009.

15. Notker Wolf visiting the Abbey of Umuoji/Nigeria, Africa in 2004.

16. Abbey of Nike in Enugu/Nigeria, Africa in 2004.

17. Notker Wolf as a tribal chief with the King of Enugu/Nigeria, Africa in 2004.

18. Monks performing a ritual dance for Abbot Primate in 2004.

19. Inauguration of the "Rason International Catholic Hospital" in North Korea in August 2005.

20. Abbot Primate with Florian, the son of the drummer of his band, in the kitchen of Saint'Anselmo in 2004.

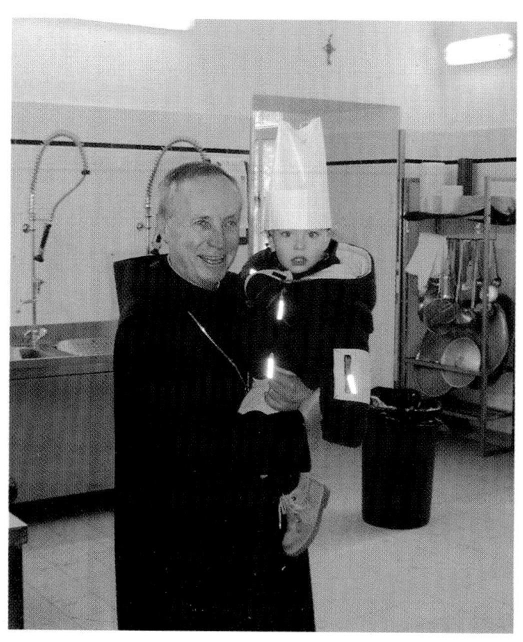

"A world without suffering and pain would be unliveable . . . because it would be without pity and compassion."

– Notker Wolf

21 & 22. Notker Wolf celebrating mass in Jillin, China in August 2005.

"Children bring a new kind of love and thus a new kind of happiness into our world."
– Notker Wolf

23. Abbot Primate with a child for bapitizing.

24. Visit to the hospital in Meihekou, China in 2005.

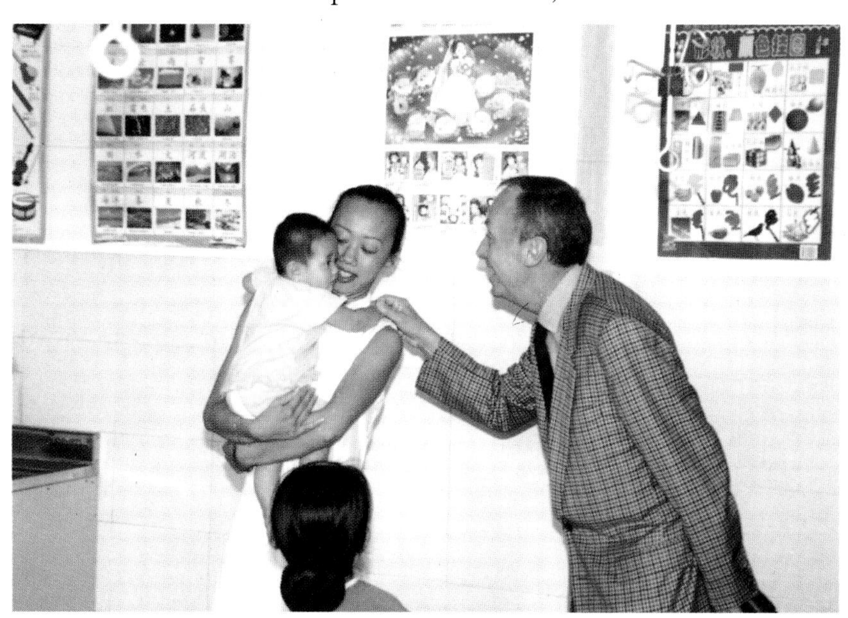

25. **"Ora et labora"**, Saint' Anselmo Rome; photo br-online in 2008.

26. Notker Wolf as Archabbot of St Ottilien preaching a sermon (photo: Rita Wolf).

27. Abbot Primate visiting Portsmouth Abbey School, USA in 2010.

28. Notker Wolf in Mount Angel/USA in 2007.

"Only someone who has questions and dares to make a new start will find his way to God, himself and other people."
– Notker Wolf

29. First canonical visitation as Archabbot in 1978 to Inkamana, Africa with Br. Clement Sithole.

30. Santo Domingo, ABECCA, excursion in 2008.

31. Notker Wolf visiting the Abbey Tepeyac, Mexico in 2005.

32 & 33. Notker Wolf taking his leave of members of the Priory in Cobán, Guatemala in 2008.

"Looking and listening to someone is a form of love."
– Notker Wolf

34. Notker Wolf visiting a convent in Cogon near Digos, Philippines in 2008.

35. Notker Wolf with Fr.Christian Temu from Tanzania in St Ottilien in 2009.

"Tolerance is seeing God's image in others."
– Notker Wolf

36. Visit with Abbot President Albert Schmidt to the nuns on Mount of Olives, Jerusalem in 2009.

37. Workshop of the American Abbots in Oceanside, California in 2010.

38. Workshop in Johannesburg, South Africa in 2010.

39. Abbot Primate visiting Madagascar in 2004.

40. Notker Wolf in conversation with His Beatitude Gregorios III Laham, Patriarch of Damascus and Beirut in 2010.

41. 1100th anniversary of Cluny, France (photo: Cluny website in 2010).

42. Visit to the Abbey Peramiho, Tanzania, Africa in 2008.

43. Notker Wolf giving a talk in the Abbey Peramiho in 2008.

This is quite a different attitude from that of prohibiting work on Sunday. As strange it as it may seem, it can bring us closer to understanding what is special about the Christian interpretation of Sunday, as well as what has gone wrong with this today.

"Prefer nothing to the work (service) of God" says Benedict. Sunday rest. Sunday duty. Day of the Lord. Is this what Sunday is about?

Perhaps we too – according to C.J. Jung – have archetypes of God in us. "In these holy halls" – we tremble before greatness and majesty. We also have the idea of "holy rest".

Rest is an important factor, even when I am talking about the Christian Sunday. But this is not the holy rest we know from other religions. It is not the rest of the Egyptian Gods, before whom the people trembled. Nor is it the sacred rest of Aristotle for whom God is the unmoved mover: a reality where nothing moves at all.

Johannes B. Metz once said that the shortest definition of religion would be "a break". What people today long for is indeed a break from the things they have to do, from the endless pressure, from the hamster wheel in which they are trapped.

Sunday in Biblical tradition is a day when you pause and rest. There should be a break from the daily stress of working life. In Genesis 34 it is written: "Six days you should work and on the seventh you should rest."

Christianity in the sense of liberation also means taking

a break from the pressure of work. I am in the midst of my everyday and work routines, and cannot totally remove myself from the real world which today is determined by work, but I am able to take a break. This shows that the claims of work are relative and that it doesn't determine everything.

So we come to the meaning and value of Sunday. I can simply shake off the pressure and the need to be constantly doing something. When speaking of the value of Sunday in a sermon during his visit to Vienna, Benedict XVI said, "The restless greediness for life which drives people today ends in the barrenness of wasted life." Sunday is an alternative to the barrenness of life wasted through hectic, restless activity.

This seems utopian in a world where money is everything. In the USA the shops are open round the clock. Twenty-four hours a day and seven days a week. And we are moving towards this in our country too. Sunday is already being increasingly eroded in our society. It will probably one day fall victim to the fanatical productivity principle of our economy. Our lives will become banal. "Banal" actually means trivial, hence ultimately meaningless.

Must we then resign ourselves? No. To put it radically, as far as I'm concerned, people should just be individualistic and work round the clock. And when they say, "But we need one day to rest, because it does us good", then I could answer, "Right. But the day of rest can be whenever you want. It doesn't have to be Sunday." I possibly have to have some kind of rhythm, like the parish priest, for example, who has every Monday off. The parish priest is doing this in principle because he works on Saturday and Sunday. If one argues thus, Sunday is not really the obligatory free day for everyone.

But the point here is not having a free day. The point is having a day free for being together with others, a day for example for the family, for the parish, for celebrating together. This is totally different from an arbitrary break from work.

A day of rest is not an adequate explanation of the meaning of Sunday. A day of rest in the week is not the equivalent of Sunday. And in our pluralistic society I can also no longer claim that Sunday, as a Christian day, should be the mandatory free day for everyone.

Of course I can also expect our pluralistic society to show consideration. When two-thirds of our society are Christians, then it is not too much to ask the remaining third to agree that Sunday is made the free day for everyone so that this section of the population can at least go to their church.

What is important is the consensus of society. It is no longer left to the discretion of the individual to choose a free day. A woman employed by a supermarket has to be on the till. Here it will certainly be necessary for society to choose a day for everyone and say let us allow everyone this day. Otherwise the unskilled workers in particular will be entirely subjected to the profit motive. Here societies must show solidarity.

In addition to the social aspect of Sunday, its spiritual significance is of course also important. This goes beyond its function of cementing society together. That is also what the common free day does. But the spiritual aspect is also connected with the experience of community.

For Christians, Sunday is the day when the resurrection is celebrated, which is why it is called the Lord's Day. I may say with a little exaggeration that I do not go to church on Sunday to pray but to celebrate together with others the mystery of our salvation. That is something quite different. To all those who say, "I do not need to go to church on Sunday, I can equally well go into the forest to pray", I say, "Firstly I do not believe that you go into the forest to pray. And secondly and even more importantly, you cannot celebrate your faith with others there." Christianity is not an individualistic solution, even though in the nineteenth century through the emergence of individualism this misinterpretation became possible. Christianity is a community of the faithful. And this becomes clear on Sunday.

The idea that Christians are primarily a community of the faithful has often unfortunately been lost, even in the church itself. Sunday has become a Sunday duty. Sunday as a rule of church has undermined the ability to hold fast to what is essential: to remember on one day of the week that Jesus has promised his presence if we commemorate the Last Supper together. You can't do this alone in your room or alone in the forest in beautiful natural surroundings. Human beings are not made so that they can find

God only for themselves. Christianity is first of all a community of the faithful as it is said today in the words of institution of the Canon, the "Mystery of faith", the communion of all the faithful. This is what Sunday is really about. This is why I celebrate the Eucharist on Sunday. It is the commemoration of God's work of salvation, of His love for us. Sunday is thus for me first of all the day of celebrating the Eucharist as part of a community.

Nowadays in a metropolis like Munich, two-thirds of the population are living as singles. How could they be expected to see the church service in terms of a genuine experience of community? I am convinced that, in an individualized society in particular, the liturgy has to offer alternative models which will once again integrate the singles. If human beings were not created to live as singles, then the church must again build communities from the base. Bringing together young and old, children and senior citizens, people from all social classes to celebrate the Eucharist on Sunday would be a real healing contribution to our society. Because the liturgy is more than pious worship.

The reason for the decreasing numbers of people who go to mass on Sunday is that there is no understanding of precisely this aspect. A law has been made out of it: on Sunday one has to go to church and pray. It is thus again turned into prohibition. We are not allowed to feel unwell or to go somewhere because on Sunday I "am obliged . . ."

And when we are "obliged" to do something, then that's the end of freedom and we rebel immediately. The deeper significance of going to church has never been made clear.

This is nothing to do with counting up how many people come to church. It is about developing a new feeling for how important it is, how existential. It is the celebration of the heart of Christianity from which I obtain the strength to master my everyday life. Christians should not be ordered through catechesis to do something, but sensitized to the fact that it is precisely this that makes them free.

In the meantime understanding of the deeper meaning of Sunday is growing. Benedict XVI reminded the congregation during Sunday mass in St Stephen's Cathedral, Vienna, that for the first Christians in ancient times, the Eucharist on Sunday was not a commandment even under the threat of death, but an inner necessity. And the Pope asked what this had to do with the Christians of our day. "A great deal", he said, and went on, "We also need a relationship which supports us, gives our life direction and content. And we need the contact with our redeemer, which supports us through death. We need this encounter which brings us together, gives us freedom and enables us to look beyond the bustle of everyday life to the creative love of God from which we come and to which we return." Sunday as the time of conscious return to this inner core – this is what we must go back to, and get away from thinking formalistically in terms of commandments.

Today we are in the same situation as the first

Christians. We must spell out Christianity afresh. The church must start right from the beginning. People must find the Christian way again. The crisis in the church is also an enormous opportunity.

I am sure the future of Christianity will also depend on the rediscovery of Sunday. When Benedict says, "Prefer nothing to the work (service) of God" then it is clear this is not a minor matter. Worship of God doesn't mean for him just the celebration of the Eucharist but in general the daily prayers of the monks in the community. Jesus ate together with His disciples. Worship doesn't mean silent adoration. It means worshipping together, a joint experience. The Greek word "Leiturgia" a combination of "laos," people, and "ergon," work, means the service of adoration which we owe God. The liturgy is the work of the people. Not the work of the individual. The experience of the Christian God – the joint liberating celebration of God and His love by the community is the real value of Sunday. It is the heart of Christianity.

The human element is also there: people's basic need to have a really refreshing rest and be free of the hectic activity which drives them during the week. The particular quality of the break in our daily life is what makes Sunday special: this is what we should restore.

In recent decades a great deal has been done to enable people to attend Sunday mass. The service has to a certain extent been brought to the people. In my childhood there was only one mass, at 9 o'clock in the morning. In winter people walked as much as two hours through the snow from the remote hamlets. It was a real community celebration which began with the rosary, and involved a long sermon and High Mass accompanied by a parish choir. Afterwards the men went for a drink, including the priest. He knew what was going on in his parish and did not have to establish an artificial closeness to his parishioners. Later there was an early mass at 7 o'clock for the housewives, so that they could prepare Sunday lunch, and then, in consideration of the new working hours of the industrial workers, the half-past ten mass, also called the "lazybones mass". Next came Sunday evening mass and finally the pre-Sunday mass on Saturday. The attempt to enable everyone to attend a Sunday mass was made to the detriment of the consciousness and experience of community. To say nothing of the burden on the priest. In the past he had one mass and two vicars to support him and today he has five masses to conduct alone and is also responsible for two other parishes which were formerly independent.

I do not harbour feelings of nostalgia. The days when our lives revolved around agriculture are past. Even the industrial society is largely a thing of the past. In times of anonymity and individualism we need new ways to build a modern consciousness of community which revolves around the Sunday Eucharist as the central celebration of faith. Parishes will then once again become the salt of the earth, the cement which holds our society together.

12 More Haste, Less Speed

AN airport is an ideal place to think – about people, about time and about life. When I get off the plane and stroll to baggage claim, taking my time over it, I see how the other passengers charge off to the conveyor belt. It is unbelievable. Everyone is in a great rush. I have the impression they don't think they are rushing. Or they don't notice it any more. And at the same time they know from experience that they are going to have to wait again whether they get there quickly or slowly.

Departure is much the same thing. When the announcement is made at the gate that "in a few minutes we will be ready for boarding", then all the passengers get up as if on command and make haste to form a queue as if they wanted to be first or were trying to get starting places for a race. Even old people who are hardly able to stand, in spite of the fact that everyone has a seat reservation, cheap flights excepted.

I remain seated and watch.

Rushing about is part of modern life. Rome, the city where I live, is a place which is hectically in motion all the time. In ancient Rome, walking slowly was a sign of freedom and dignity. Only a slave ran. There was a feeling for the dignity of slowness.

In his economic history of modern capitalism, Werner Sombart cites a fifteenth-century Florentine merchant who said he had never seen a hard-working person who did not walk slowly. Slowness was once a form of strength and security, an expression of stability.

That is no longer the case. People seem to have lost this inner stability. The tempo of the world today is globally driven. Nothing is as it was in the past. Managers who are inwardly driven by a task move faster than ordinary workers. This applies all over the world: Asia too is by no means a meditative continent where people live at a slower and more thoughtful pace, and the streets of Asian metropolises everywhere present the same picture. The Japanese rush about, push and run, and so do the Chinese and Koreans. And if you ever travel in Kerala in India by bus or car, you will wish you had made your last confession.

Scientific studies have been carried out to measure and compare walking speeds. It has been found that people on the streets of Freiburg walk more slowly than people in Düsseldorf. And if you have ever been to New York and are familiar with Greece, it will not astonish you to hear that New Yorkers walk twice as fast as Greek farmers. They also speak more quickly and their facial expressions change more rapidly and are generally more mobile. And it will scarcely come as a surprise that people in the city of Hamburg are faster than farmers who work according to a natural rhythm. A farmer from the Allgäu is never in a hurry, and says tomorrow is another day. A farmer from Upper Bavaria will also resist pressure. Young farmers may perhaps see things a little differently, but will also strongly resist unnecessary pressure to speed things up.

Some people are only able to rush. They cannot stand still any more. When I am in a rush it means I am having to do something faster than I want to. And even worse, I am doing it faster than I am able. What is behind all this hurry? I suspect fear. Fear of not being able to finish everything in time in a limited lifespan. Or the fear of coming off badly. Or perhaps the fear of being punished by the person who is forcing me to do something. When I myself am in a hurry and someone suddenly holds me up and forces me to listen to him I may react a little grumpily. But basically the pause is even good for me.

On the wall of a coffeehouse in Vienna is the saying "I won't be hurried, I'm not running away from anything." Flight is the result of fear that somebody will use violence on me. Our running, rushing and hurrying has to do with fear.

The feeling for the dignity of slowness in our fast-paced times has gone out of fashion. You can still see this deliberate slowness in the monasteries when the monks enter the church. The slow pace at which this procession moves is the opposite of rushing.

When I walk at this speed, I am giving myself space as well as making room for emotion. Someone rushing gives me the impression of instability and insecurity. Even fear. Treading slowly and with dignity is not only appropriate for a sacred building or a church service. Baroque dances such as the minuet and sarabande also reflect this: when the dancers enter they also proceed at this slow pace. And this was also incidentally the practice at court when the king arrived, which is why I am rather wary of over-exaggerating this movement. When I enter the church then it is at a steady, not too fast pace, with measured steps but with a natural, normal rhythm.

The most important thing for me is that a dignified, measured pace is an expression of the knowledge that we have a regal dignity. We Christians can walk with our heads in the air because we have an inner freedom, our value does not depend on others who define and drive us, but we have an inner dignity. That is right for us, that is our nature and how we were meant to be. We move harmoniously: "moderate" is not without reason also a tempo found in music.

Getting away from the fast pace of life, leaving time behind us with all the demands it imposes from outside, and ceasing from being driven – this is what music expresses for me with its inner flow. The Gregorian chants focus on mystery and renounce haste. They are like an artist applying his paints.

Last year I spent my holidays by a lake. When I walked around the lake every morning, I saw people jogging and torturing themselves with their early morning sport. Out of twenty people there was perhaps only one who was walking normally. I am no jogging expert, but these poor people were driven by an obsession with health or wellness. I felt sorry for them. If they had moved at a more relaxed pace it would have certainly done them more good than this obsessiveness. At any rate, it looked more tortured and driven than anything else.

We are often driven. Even in our free time we need action. When time stops and I am fully aware of the present, it brings me face to face with myself. Someone who is afraid of working on and becoming aware of himself, will try to "distract" himself. Very few people are able to tolerate themselves. My old prior used to say that the hardest thing for the novices was learning how to tolerate themselves.

When time standing still is perceived as boredom, then it is necessary to distract oneself. The person who lives in the present and tolerates time no longer has to hurry. He is simply *there.*

13 Meditation is Being Fully There

"IT'S strange that we talk of "driving away" (vertreiben) the time" says Rilke. "The problem is more one of how to hold on to it." How apt those words are today. Distraction is a basic evil of our time. Simple and pious people often used to confess, "I have prayed inattentively." Elderly people in particular complain of absent-mindedness. But that is not what I mean when I say that our culture is a culture of distraction.

Concentration and paying attention to something are becoming more and more difficult. People who watch television will be used to the simultaneous transmission of different pieces of information, which is actually distracting our attention. Whether it is the Deutsche Welle or CNN, the film on the screen is undertitled with another item of news. The picture shows the Dalai Lama arriving in Berlin, while the latest stock market prices glide past along the bottom of the screen.

And this disturbs us.

We do have the ability to do two or three things at the same time. Sometimes it is even useful. But talking to somebody and doing something else at the same time is quite unacceptable.

This is also the whole point of meditation: *being totally there*. It is of course not easy and there is no method which makes it happen. We Germans think we can make everything happen. That is erroneous. Some things have to develop in a natural way. Education, for example, is something that is acquired gradually. And meditation is just the same.

I am repeatedly asked what Benedictine meditation is. People think that there will be a special method, perhaps even a form of efficient instruction. The opposite is the case. It is not a method, it is a way of life. It is the balance acquired through the daily alternation of prayer and work. This balance, this rhythm is of course also internalized if it is experienced every day, and goes deeper and deeper into the individual. If somebody consistently lives the life of a monk, then after 30 years he is certainly not the same person he was as a novice. But that is not achieved through a particular method, through headstands or tricks.

Someone for whom activity and prayer belong together and who engages in both every day, will be changed through the power of this practice. Silence, which is not empty silence and is much more than doing nothing, goes very well with an active life.

There is a story about a young novice and his novice master which relates how the novice, who was not exactly diligent, complained that he had not yet experienced the silence his novice master was recommending. His master's answer was, "Only active people experience silence."

Of course there are methods of meditation which people can learn and practise. All these do is help you become calmer and perhaps also concentrate better. But I think the spirituality of a Christian discussion goes deeper. Its "result" is achieving total presence.

Gregory the Great described being a monk as "residing in yourself". Zen Buddhism has this too. A person practising *zazen* sits in silence and concentrates on his breath. Then time stands still and he feels its presence and its passing as he breathes. But he does not experience this as something negative, he gives himself up to this rhythm of nature and of the cosmos. It is virtually an experience of depersonalization. All ideas and emotions are extinguished.

In my opinion Christianity and Christian meditation are different. They involve a personal relationship. For Christians the greatest thing is to become one with God as an individual person. And God does not let me enter a Nirvana but first brings me to completion as a person. I can anchor myself in Him. He gives me my dignity and my peace. I don't have to rush around or allow myself to be driven by others. In God's presence too I find eternity.

Christian meditation is not designed for improving one's own abilities. It is always related to God and to people. Some people say my interpretation is too concrete. I can only answer that love is always concrete. It is related to another person. And the heart of Christianity is really love. This has consequences for the way we treat each other. It means, for example, saying now nothing else is important, I am only here for you. I must consciously make myself free for the other person. I must take the time for this, or as far as I'm concerned steal it if necessary.

Giving someone our full attention shows us that we can experience a different quality of time, which is not normal time as it is counted in hours and minutes. It is an experience of eternity.

How I can explain this experience of eternity?

I cannot do this.

Nor can I explain the difference between red and green.

I can perhaps explain the wave length but not the quality of the colour. This you have to see.

And you also cannot explain the experience of eternity.

You have to experience it for yourself.

14 Presence: Happiness is when Time Stands Still

In Arthur Miller's play "Death of a Salesman", there is a scene which I can still remember today, even though it's a very long time since I saw the production. The scene takes place in the first act. Willy Lohmann, the hero, is talking to his wife Linda and at the same time remembering another woman. His thoughts and feelings are elsewhere while he is talking to Linda. During their conversation someone can be seen walking backwards and forwards in the background. The woman he is really thinking about is already visible. She is the one who is really present for him.

The scene disturbed me at the time. In the meantime I have realized that it is a sign and disease of the times. A cartoon in the "New Yorker" expresses this very well. First there is a scene of a man sitting behind his desk with a thought bubble that shows he is imagining how nice it would be to be playing golf. In the next picture he is playing golf and the thought bubble shows him thinking about a woman. The final picture shows him in bed with a woman and in his head at this moment is an image of his desk . . . He is never where he actually is and where he should be. He is always somewhere else instead of coming to a stop and being present.

Perhaps that's why this scene in Arthur Miller's play disturbed me so much, because I realized I am sometimes guilty of the same thing. I have experienced this form of inattention in myself time and again. I have been talking to someone and my thoughts have been elsewhere. It is good then when the person in question tells you the truth and says, "You're not with me at all." You are there but you are not listening and are not taking in what the other person is saying. I have sometimes been pulled up sharply for this. Women in particular react very sensitively. This also applies to making a phone call and glancing at the newspaper at the same time. It can be hard to have it pointed out. But it is quite right.

Attention is what matters when you are really having a conversation. A conversation is time spent with another person. And when you are with another person, you must not be somewhere else. Presence takes place with all the senses. That is what being *totally there* means. There is no room for anything else. *Attention* means this and nothing else. Some people iron, listen to the radio and at the same time watch everything going on in the street. Others can read and listen to music at the same time. I am not talking about multitasking of this kind. A youngster can of course also be so totally "present" in a killing game on the computer that he gets lost in it. But that is not fulfilled time.

To give attention to somebody without being distracted is a form of politeness, but it is more than this: it also has a spiritual aspect and a seriousness that has nothing to do with convention. Although we should be careful about how we use the term spiritual, someone once said that the real art of living consisted of seeing what was wonderful about everyday things. Perhaps what is meant by the spiritual quality of attention and presence is that in the middle of what you are doing time stands still.

There are very intensive moments in which we are so fully with someone or immersed in something that we forget the time and have the feeling that time is standing still. We are simply present. The philosopher Boethius sees eternity as a kind of all-encompassing present.

It could not be put better. Even when I really love a person, it can still happen that other worries are bothering me at the same time or I am under time pressure. But when this person is with me nothing else counts. Everything else has to be stopped. If I do not have this attitude then I should not give this person my attention. Semi-attention is not right.

To give someone the gift of time means to take him seriously. It is not just being polite as required by social convention. Conventional politeness or a social conversation may require omitting topics which are actually important. But a real conversation always involves being truthful. I must be truthful too. Of course I must never beat someone over the head with the truth. But if I don't tell him the truth then I am not taking him seriously, I am not expecting anything from him. Telling the truth gives a real conversation weight. And such a conversation requires trust. And needs time.

Time is money, so the saying goes. A time researcher has changed this sentence into time is honey. Time is like honey when it is spent with other people. It will then flow more slowly, it will be sweet and enjoyable. Spending time with others is indeed one of the best things I can think of: conversing over a good meal and a glass of good wine. There doesn't even have to be anything on the table. And anyhow rather nothing than an unappetizing meal. A good wine also has to be drunk thoughtfully and slowly. Wine also involves time. As does a person who is telling me his story. But nothing else is important, only the person. And it is wonderful to have time for someone and to be there for him.

I can say nothing better to a friend than "Never mind the time, it's *you* that's important." In Büchner's comedy "Leonce and Lena", a play about love, it says, "We shall have all clocks smashed, all calendars banned, and count hours and moons only by the flower clock, only by the flowers and fruits." Not looking at your watch, not allowing yourself to be pressurized from outside is a symbol of love. And actually also a symbol of attention to each individual. I do have small clocks on my desk and bookshelf that I can glance at discreetly so that I don't neglect other obligations because of this particular conversation. But in practice I don't look at them. I simply forget.

You cannot count every minute when nursing a sick

person. Attention cannot be measured with a stopwatch and nursing is not an activity carried out on the assembly line principle. Measurement of the time devoted to someone is measurement of the soul. Its criterion is the heart. In no way is one always only the giver. On the contrary. My key experience was when I once went to see a sick brother in the monastery with whom I actually had very little contact. He was considered to be a difficult person. I had decided not to stay too long, and it was more a duty or routine visit. And then suddenly, as I was already saying goodbye, he asked, "Have you got another couple of minutes?" Of course I had. These two minutes became two hours. A whole life was revealed. In these two hours my fellow monk opened up as he had never done before. And it happened once again that the time offered became a gift to the giver. I was the one who went away a changed person. For me it was a Copernican turning point. Since this day I know with certainty that when I get involved with somebody and take time, what I get back cannot be measured in terms of time. In these moments I must not look at the clock. When the other person is there, he is there.

It does not bother me at all, if I occasionally miss something which is apparently very important. Of course it can happen. Up to now I have rarely missed an appointment, but when it really does happen then I say, "Oh well." As it says at the end of Hebbel's play "Agnes Bernauer": "It would have been so beautiful, so it was not to be."

Visitors sometimes say to me, "You give the impression of having all the time in the world."

"My answer is then, "Now it's you who are important and no one else."

The fact that my desk is covered with papers is another matter. But this is not so important at this moment. Afterwards I will reshuffle my priorities. And keep my e-mail replies a bit shorter.

15 The Right Moment

AT the beginning of the Rule of Benedict it says, "Listen my son, to the precepts of the master and incline the ear of your heart." "Heart" means empathy. It is the organ of empathy for others. But it also means awareness for the Law of the Lord and how it is to be applied in a concrete situation. Awareness for another person, awareness of the moment and a joint feeling for the right moment to act, all this belongs together.

It says in the chapter about the duties of the abbot that "The Abbot should have a feeling for the right moment." Given that people are different, Benedict says that their individual characters must be taken into consideration by the person who is leading them. When you read his Rule, you get an idea of the kinds of people who were living in his community: there were stubborn, gloomy and headstrong individuals, and even people with designs on the lives of others. The abbot, said Benedict, should treat everyone gently and individually. He should urge willing individuals to make a little more effort, and show the incorrigible how to behave by his own example. Many abbots who complain about the members of their communities today would not say another word if they really thought about the range of characters Benedict had to deal with. Everyone was to be respected and loved equally.

"One word at the wrong time is like meat without salt", it says in the Wisdom of Jesus, son of Sirach in the Old Testament. Anyone who ever has eaten a bland or oversalted meal knows what this means. If you turn the sentence around it also has a message: being aware of the right moment and making use of it gives spice to life.

"There is also a special time for acting", says Qohelet. But what the right moment is cannot be determined from outside. It will always depend on the particular situation, on the particular state, possibilities, will and intentions of the individual.

I experienced how important the right time is in the case of a young man doing community service with us. His grandmother had been very ill for two years and had suffered considerably. A medical examination showed that she was in the final stages of cancer. Because I felt how important his grandmother was to him, I told the young man to go home. He went home to Berlin and was able to be present at her death. She was in a palliative ward, had no pain and played the piano for him every day. After one week she was able to die – because her grandson was there.

Acting at the right moment sometimes means acting fast. But sometimes it also means being able to wait. However, this waiting is a form of being prepared or aware, it is not passive waiting. The art of leading does not consist of permanent intervention, but of being aware, present and "nearby" if people need you – and recognizing at the right moment when you really are needed. Of course I talk to people, but I must wait for the moment when I am really needed.

When this comes, I must not look at my watch or think of my next appointment, no, then I must stop everything else I am doing.

Being aware is being ready. With children you have to wait and watch. But when they have a particular need then they need your attention *now* and the problem that is troubling them has to be sorted out *immediately* and not the day after tomorrow.

It was always like this. If somebody comes to me and asks, "Have you got a minute?" and I feel it is something really important for him but with the best will in the world I am not free at that moment, then it is essential to arrange another time the same day or on the day after. Everyone understands if right now is not possible. But the problem is there *today* and will perhaps be there tomorrow as well. Postponing the solution or clarification beyond this narrow time frame can sometimes mean it is too late. Then a situation may have become irreversible. Sometimes you can let things blow over. And sometimes the best thing to do in the case of a problem is to sleep on it. But it should never simply be ignored if this is the moment when something should be sorted out.

A beautifully formulated and very humane approach is to be found in ancient monastic tradition. It was supported by Cassian, the monk and theologian who was born in the fourth century and whose thinking influenced Benedict. He too takes his cue from Qohelet: "Everything has its time." But he goes on to say that nothing has an abstract value. Nothing is fixed for ever. "Everything can change for better or worse. Nothing is either good or bad in itself." Behind this is a great trust in and an enormous sympathy for people. Nobody is judged from the outset. Someone who wants to grab everything for himself, says Cassian, can become someone who can let go, and an oversensitive person can turn into someone who overcomes difficulties.

The same thought is behind Benedict's statement that seeing the particular quality of a moment and recognizing the right time is not a matter of calculation but of wisdom or perception on the part of the individual. I must, for example, know when the other person is able to bear the truth. And I must know when I must expect him to do so. It is not however right if I cannot expect anything of the other person, I must be able to expect something of him.

Nothing is fixed forever, many things are possible. We must be aware of this. The ancient Greek word for the right moment is "kairos". That is exactly what cannot be mastered with time management. It is awareness of the given situation and of what is needed which leads to the "right moment".

There are right and wrong times. I can tackle someone at the wrong time. And I must not say everything on every occasion.

The most important thing is always the welfare of the individual. The abbot must remember this and understand that the person is not there because of the Rule. The duty of the leader is to apply the Rule according to the situation.

Consistent decision-making based on people's welfare is what makes a good leader. This is also what I expect from a good manager: Sovereignty and a feeling for the right moment. A manager must be able to let things go because he knows they are being dealt with by others. He must have an overview and know when he has to do something himself. He does not have to control every little thing. He must however understand that he is not the most important person. Others are also important and some feel called to perform particular tasks. These people must be given the possibility to prove themselves. Most of them also carry out these tasks well. Leading means encouraging people and helping them develop.

For many highly-placed managers, fast and efficient action now takes priority over people's welfare. Self-assertion and toughness are the prized virtues. Many managers concentrate solely on organizational and financial matters. How people feel is secondary. Someone who has no relationship to people and no longer sees the consequences of this has lost sight of the human dimension.

In the chapter of his Rule that deals with the appointment and the service of an abbot Benedict says, "He is not to be turbulent and anxious, nor excessive and stubborn, nor jealous and over-suspicious, for then he is never at rest."

The feeling for the right moment can also involve setting limits. This means developing a feeling for when one doesn't want to be monopolized. When problems should be left where they belong. This also has to do with making proper use of your time. Perhaps it is also good time management not to try and be involved with everything. When people want to push something onto me, people who like to delegate everything "upwards", or simply want me to get involved in a particular issue, then I am not afraid to say, no, that is your responsibility. I do not say this to save myself time. I don't save time in this way but I don't get involved with everything. This is what the subsidiarity principle is all about.

The biblical saying that there is a right time for every happening and for every action applies to all of us. The art lies in realizing what is right when and for whom. And then doing what one has to do.

It is as simple as that.

And as important in life as the salt in the soup.

16 Learning how to Wait

I LEARNED how to wait.

Mostly at airports.

Anyone who has to sit around at airports as often as I have knows what it is like to see time running away. For example when the plane is delayed. Or if you have to wait a whole hour in the plane when nothing is happening. In such situations I get impatient too and feel like grinding my teeth.

But then I quickly conclude that there is nothing I can do about it.

I must keep cool.

I mustn't get excited.

I must remain absolutely calm.

This is the most important thing when you are forced to wait, to say to yourself there is nothing you can do about it.

Once in such a situation before departure at the airport in Paris I met the former Cardinal Ratzinger. Our plane was delayed by more than an hour. He and his companion were reading and I sat down elsewhere. I didn't want to disturb him – I don't like being disturbed in such situations either. So we waited. Eventually we did arrive in Rome. After landing we were standing at baggage claim and that always takes a long time in Rome. The luggage finally came and mine was first. I said, "Eminence, look, my luggage is here already. I have to fly such a lot, if you only knew how many hours I have spent waiting! But now I think I have found a reason to believe in indulgences again. I am counting on the whole time that I will have spent waiting at airports in the course of my life being deducted from my time in purgatory." "That's a very strange theory", he replied. "But a good one", I answered with a grin.

There is nothing for it. When there is no way round it you must simply get something good out of waiting. Once, for example, I was trying to buy a train ticket in China. We stood in a long queue in front of the ticket office. And waited and waited. Finally it was our turn, and when we asked for our ticket the reply was, "For foreigners? Upstairs!"

So up we went and stood at the back of another queue. When we got to the front we were told, "Oh you've only got foreign currency, please go over there."

And the same process began all over again.

What should you do? It used to be possible to smoke a pipe everywhere and that was once again my salvation. With a pipe I have no problem waiting. I watch the smoke and enjoy its constant slow movement. There is nothing better.

And when I sit, for example in a waiting room, and observe others coming in and also waiting, somehow time stands still. Or at least slows down, which is splendid. Then I can wait for hours. Since smoking is no longer allowed in airports, the only help is to pray. When I now wait in a long queue at security control at Fiumencino airport in Rome, have nobody to talk to and can't do anything, then I take out my rosary. Pious people would say it's about time!

Waiting has two sides to it.

There is empty waiting without a real aim, without anticipation and without hope.

But there is also fulfilled waiting. In the tradition of the monks, waiting has just this meaning. The hermits in the desert, who waited under the most inhospitable conditions, were not waiting for the fulfilment of a special wish or to attain a particular goal. Their "waiting for God" was something that freed them from their own expectations and opened their hearts for the one who is "greater than our hearts". They were fulfilled by waiting.

And there is a lovely kind of waiting. When children wait for Santa Claus during Advent or for the Easter bunny in spring. And even if the Christmas gift does not perhaps quite come up to expectations, no one can take away the anticipation.

The man waiting for his girlfriend also experiences a joyful tension as he anticipates her coming. Anticipation is something wonderful. When a mother carrying a small child waits at arrivals and the child wriggles with anticipation when he sees daddy coming through the barrier, that is something I love to see and I share their pleasure. Such waiting is the fulfilment of a relationship. While I am longing for someone they are already present. That is the joy of waiting.

It is also necessary to be able to wait for something and not have every desire fulfilled immediately; your enjoyment of the desired object will then be all the greater. It is splendid when you are out hiking and approach a restaurant. One ad says that "Beer needs thirst", and the wise Montaigne once said, "Whoever doesn't wait until he's thirsty to drink will not find drinking pleasurable." Pleasure is the reward for asceticism. Waiting also often increases motivation. For example, when I set out to climb a mountain I can see the summit. The ascent is before me, but the path to the top is already part of the goal. It is already a kind of arrival, even if it is going to take a long time. I am happy when I see the top from afar and waiting is part of the achievement. Prolonging the satisfaction of desire is altogether an important ascetic principle. It makes us prudent and free. Caesar used to count to twenty before he reacted.

Waiting is connected with patience. When people ask me if it is possible to learn patience I answer, "Some have it by nature and the others have to learn it." But it can be worked at. Someone once said that it takes a lot of patience to learn to be patient. Nevertheless, the person who works at being patient will probably also gradually find it easier. Those who always had to wait as children and were not immediately granted every wish will find it easier to practise this virtue in difficult life situations.

Wanting to have everything simultaneously and immediately is a widespread attitude today. But it won't get you very far in life. Being patient is not always wanting to have everything immediately. Being able to wait and be patient also means first being able to do without something. How can we help children acquire this ability? No sweet without sweat. That's what we learned at school and it didn't do us any harm. If a young person wants to get on in life, he must learn how to do without. This was the mistake made by the generation influenced by the events of 1968. They wanted to bring their children up in such a way that they never had to experience frustration. But frustration and disappointment are part of every life. The important thing is not to throw in the towel the moment difficulties are encountered.

Patience means being able to see time passing without getting frustrated or aggressive. Patience means being able to put up with something and say to yourself that it will come to an end. Waiting is bearable when you know that a great deal can be achieved with time.

But it doesn't just mean putting your hands in your lap, quite the opposite. Nor does it mean just waiting for success. You have to do something while you are waiting for success. "What are we waiting for?" is the signal for purposeful activity.

Being patient, taking time, thus does not mean doing nothing and waiting for others to act instead of you. Taking time means being able to wait in order to make a development possible, to let something grow. Attentiveness, vigilance, support – all this is part of patience.

We know from the Bible that patience is a divine virtue. In the Old Testament, God is the forbearing, the patient and the merciful one and sets man an example of loyalty. In the New Testament Jesus tells the parable of the farmer who sows his seeds and doesn't immediately pull up the weeds someone has sown in his wheat. Because God has patience with us we also shouldn't be too quick to immediately demand the best of others. Even if it takes time, we should give the other person space to develop and find his own way.

Patience has its opposites: impatience and longing.

Impatience is not only the edginess which is the opposite of calm. There is also a lovely impatience, as when you are going to see somebody you have always wanted to meet for the first time. Then you can hardly wait, and it is a heavenly kind of impatience.

Longing is something special. Longing for someone is not the same thing as boredom.

Longing is part of life, like waiting for fulfilment. But being bored is something quite different.

I have never succeeded in being bored, not even at school.

"Let's wait" was always my maxim. And when I see something has to be done I still tend to ask, "What are we waiting for?"

17 When Time is Hell

THERE is a kind of waiting that seems endless. I associate this with the experience of night. In a world where night has been turned into day, we often forget that the natural way of looking at night is in terms of threat and danger. In many parts of the world where the technical resources for overcoming darkness are lacking, night is still not a good time. It is the time without light or heat. The time when life retreats, when colour is no longer visible and when the structure and order of the world seems to disappear.

The Bible also talks about this original human experience: man is threatened by the powers of darkness. It is not only the experience of an age long past. The night service of the monks includes a reading from the first letter of Peter: "Be calm but vigilant, because your enemy the devil is prowling round like a roaring lion, looking for someone to eat. Stand up to him, strong in faith."

I know what I am talking about. When you are ill in bed, the night never seems to end. I know what it is like to toss and turn and be unable to sleep. You count every quarter of an hour and time moves with painful slowness.

You hear every chime. It is a depressing, black endlessness. You wait, knowing that waiting is pointless.

In such a night of dark thoughts it is not even helpful to count sheep. When you try to count to 1000, you soon return to your previous chain of thought. Praying the rosary doesn't help either, since you can't pray 376 rosaries one after another.

This is what I imagine hell, or at any rate purgatory to be like: a night that one longs to be over but never is. The existential play by Jean-Paul Sartre "No Exit" describes people who have been shut up with one another and who tear one another apart. For me this is comparable with the experience of a sick and lonely person who lies isolated in his bed and cannot get to sleep. Being alone in such a situation when time does not pass and there is no hope of change, that is hell.

Time is honey – this does not apply when you are sick. Time is no longer sweet, but bitter and poisonous when the minutes are infinite and the hour hand doesn't move.

Time then expands endlessly, has no structure and ceases to flow. Here the experience of eternity is a negative one.

There is music that is so beautiful and harmonious that, however long it is, we never want it to end, like Schubert's Great C major Symphony – and how wonderful this is too. But something can go on forever which neither makes sense nor gives much joy. Alfred Kerr once wrote a review of a particularly boring and excruciating play in which he said, "When I looked at my watch after two hours only twenty minutes had passed." But even the most boring play has an interval, and if it has irritated you, you can leave and find something more entertaining to do. A sleepless sick person does not have this option. Insomnia can be a torture. It is scarcely surprising that in ancient times and the Middle Ages it was used as a means of torture – and still is even now. (Although today sleep deprivation is also used for treating depression).

What can you do on such nights in your sick bed? At the most you can doze and try to endure the time passively. You can only allow time to elapse and endeavour to tolerate it. Time becomes a torture.

Positively experienced time always has prospects. With no such prospects, I have no idea how things are going to continue. Someone who has hope can get up. But someone who is sick at night cannot get up. He is doomed to be unhappy. Lying awake at night is pure desolation. This is quite different from the boredom that comes from not knowing how to fill one's time.

"Awaiting the morning" in the middle of the night is something different. There is a wonderful passage in Psalm 130:6: "My soul waits for the Lord more than watchmen for the morning, more than watchmen for the morning." Someone has kept watch all night and is happy to see dawn break at last. Thus everyone who does night duty looks forward to the coming day. A sick person, who can only wait, sees it differently.

But even that can sometimes take a turn for the good. Even insomnia can cease to be a misfortune. On one occasion I had been in a hospital on the Tiber Island in Rome for three weeks, and I could no longer sleep. The man in the bed next to me was elderly and had had a prostate operation. In this hospital the relatives had to watch over the patients at night. His wife always fell asleep. So I told her to go home and I would look after her husband. She went home after I promised her I would keep awake the whole night. And I enjoyed it. In spite of my sleeplessness it was a fulfilled time. I knew I could be there for the other person. I enjoyed it and the other person slept.

And when the night still seems long, one thing remains, hope for the next day. Even when the hours do not seem to pass, we know there will be a new day and can approach it in the hope that then everything will be better, that our health will improve or that a new working day will distract us.

"The night has twelve hours/then day will be here." These lines from the poem "Song of the Moldau" by Bert Brecht echo the spirit and the wisdom of the Bible. What it expresses is the hope that whoever waits and gives the night meaning by being there for others, will also overcome the dark side of night: consciously being with one another and there for one another is one way to drive out the demons of darkness.

18 Night Owls and Morning Larks

THE writer Karl Kraus must have worked at night. Otherwise he would not had described night work as the "victory of the spirit over the mattress". I can understand him well. I myself am a night person. Sometimes I say to myself, you chose the wrong profession. Monks usually get up very early. This is hard for someone who is a night person. In the morning the others emerge bright and breezy, whistling cheerfully. The impression I probably make on others in the morning is one of wanting to be left in peace. If I am in German company I usually even say, "Please leave me alone, I am still grouchy."

It is simply a fact. God created owls and larks. And He created the same categories of human being. That's why we have night persons and morning persons. It is not without reason that behaviourists call them "night owls" and "morning larks".

It makes sense. The night can also be a time of undistracted creativity. The distractions, exertions and tension of your everyday work are left behind and you are totally focused. *Ora et labora* is something that for me never stops.

What I don't do is worry at night and toss and turn. In Italy there is a saying that night is the blotting paper for worries. When I was elected Abbot Primate, an abbot said to me, "When you go to bed at night, leave all your worries in front of the bedroom door." And really nothing is solved by brooding over it the whole night. Someone who sleeps over – not with – his problems may well feel better the next day.

What the day has brought is not over in the evening. The day is actually always too short for me. For this reason alone I catch up at night with the things I had no time for during the day. But also, if I can't sleep at night, I get up again instead of continuing to toss and turn. I know from experience that it's no use staying in bed. For example, when I cannot sleep the first few nights after a long flight because of jetlag, then I get up in the middle of the night and open my breviary. I pray the psalms of the Vigil and meditate on the readings for this hour – and I take pleasure in finally having the opportunity to do this undisturbed. These are the hours when even the noisy city of Rome is silent and I can do what is really important for me. It is something beautiful.

One of the psalms says: "Ponder in your own hearts on your beds, and be silent" (Psalm 4:5). And in Psalm 63:7 it says: "When I remember you upon my bed and meditate on you in the watches of the night." Sleeplessness can be turned into a spiritual exercise and a way of regaining stillness. Night becomes a period of intensive prayer. And that does one a world of good.

Night is not only a time of demons but also a time of God, when He speaks to people in a special way. He speaks in the still of the night, even though we do not always hear and understand Him immediately, like the young Samuel. He wakes up in the night and hears a voice calling his name. Thinking it is his teacher Eli, he runs to him and wakes him up, saying, "You called me, here I am." Eli, however, is in a deep sleep and says, probably irritably, "No, I didn't call you, go back to bed." This happens two more times. It is only when it happens the fourth time that Samuel, encouraged by Eli, answers, "Yes Lord, here I am, please speak . . ." The story is related in Samuel 3:1-10. The Evangelist Luke describes how Jesus went up a mountain to pray and spent the whole night in prayer. Jesus repeatedly retired to pray at night, to be entirely with his heavenly father.

However, for the ancient monks the night was nevertheless more a place of darkness where the devil ruled, and it was only when the day dawned that the good angels came and led people back into life.

Prayer is thus, in the tradition of the monks, a way of turning the night into a time of God as well. For the Vigil, the night prayer, the monks got up in the middle of the night. When I open the breviary myself at 2 o'clock in the morning and begin to pray, I smile to myself because I do not have to get up.

Sometimes, in spite of all the work I have to get through every day, I have to go to a dinner or another evening invitation to fulfil certain obligations arising from my position. When I then return at 11 o'clock at night and have the feeling that it makes no sense to go to bed now, I won't be able to get to sleep anyway, it sometimes happens that I am able to work again and I usually also get fresh inspiration. Then my thoughts flow freely. It is a time free of pressure to produce something, a time in which I have space to breathe.

And then I read something or work through the mountain of papers on my desk. For a long time on such nights I used to write e-mails, in order to get them out of the way. I don't do that any more, because people see the time. Then they get a shock and react with concern. It was great to get up in the middle of the night once a week and write all my e-mails. I can also send them at 7 o'clock but not at 3 o'clock in the morning, I now have to be more careful.

I often think of that wonderful verse in the Bible: "A capable wife who can find? Her lamp does not go out at night. She puts her hands to the distaff, and her hands hold the spindle. She looks after the family." "She rises while it is yet night and provides food for the household." (Prov. 31:10). Care means giving your time to others. This quote always impresses me: while the others are sleeping, she works. And I sometimes think of this when I am still working at one-thirty in the morning. Then I am at peace with myself.

I can use the night as a time which has nothing to do with the day and its troubles. It is a free space. It is also a time when people no longer ring up, when no one knocks at the door, when I come to myself, and all the things that prevent this during the day no longer disturb me. I light a candle and its even flame and soft light create an atmosphere of beneficial peace.

There is usually a lot of outstanding work on my desk. In the past I sometimes used to clear it off in a single night. Especially when I had to fly somewhere the next day, I would sit down in the evening and in the morning my desk would be clear and I could set off without a care in the world.

I don't now have the energy I once had. And I now have to learn, over and again, to cope with that. The work will be still there when I get back.

There is another Italian saying: "Whoever does not honour the night is not worthy of the day." There are different ways of interpreting this. What is certain is that if you wake up tired in the morning and have no energy to tackle the day, that is not good.

As a night person, I could of course sleep in in the morning if I have worked through the night. But to sleep till 8 o'clock in the morning is not possible given the daily rhythm of monastery life.

And if I did, I would also be dissatisfied because I had not started the morning properly. Then all kinds of things would have piled up for me to do in the meantime. I would in addition have too little time for my spiritual contemplation. When I get up in the morning at around 6 o'clock I use the time to pray, I celebrate mass and meditate.

What does me particularly good in the morning is the silence. And I am not the only one who benefits from this. When I was first elected Abbot Primate, the monks at Sant'Anselmo tended to speak during breakfast. I insisted that the time of silence was upheld. Thank goodness. We spend the first part of the day after mass, and also while we are breakfasting together, in silence. This time of silence is my breathing space. And this carries me through the rest of the day. Breathing spaces and energy go together and that is why the day should start in this way. It is important that we don't immediately go flat out. We must first allow ourselves some peace.

"Please leave me in peace, I'll join you shortly."

That is my motto early in the morning.

At 8 o'clock the day can start.

And then I can also go flat out.

19 Squandered Time

THE former Benedictine monastery of St Peter in the southern part of the Black Forest above Freiburg, where the founder of St Ottilien, Abbot Andreas Amrhein, was ordained, still has a gallery of abbots which documents the history of the monastery. Those who know something about this and look more closely will notice that two abbots are missing. Experts in the history of St Peter explain that these abbots were not theologically unsound, nor reputed to have been guilty of questionable moral conduct. They were the abbots who had ruined the monasteries economically during their time. What this says is that an abbot is a good abbot when he actively protects and maintains the available resources. When he uses his time properly and takes responsibility.

Life is now. Time is lost when I don't see what has to be done today and take advantage of what the present has to offer. When I lose contact with life in the here and now.

People who behave in this way are daydreamers. They are not satisfied with the present, but they don't do anything about it.

Others manage their time no better, for example those who think they will lose out if they do not fill the day with activities, and rush from one event to the next or have to keep up with all the latest trends. They are simply wasting their lives.

Then there are those who cannot detach themselves from the past and are permanently trapped in it. And those who also escape the present, but by projecting all their worries, desires and hopes into the future instead. The person who clings to tomorrow will also lose today.

All the above are avoiding their responsibilities: time must be used for doing something productive.

"Your money or your life?" No one usually hesitates over the answer. Time is more valuable than money. But the sentence "time is money" can also be seen positively. Not as a financial statement but as a description of the fact that time is a precious gift which is not available forever. "Time is precious" doesn't mean that my bank account has to increase continuously. A successful businessman once said, "It is not my aim in life to be the richest person in the cemetery." My life is really precious because I can make use of the opportunity to do something creative by furthering the lives of others, by using my abilities to the benefit of the community and by helping to do something good for others and shaping our common life. My life has value in that I am able to do something in the time I am here which has a continuing effect. It is only possible while I have this time. Then it is over. That is not something I am complaining about. Then it is the turn of others.

We must not waste time or steal it from others – by

stopping them from working with idle chat. The things which should make our life easier can also steal our time. Modern technology, even computers which make our life faster and are supposed to make our work easier, are among them. When I go on the Internet to read my e-mails while travelling, I often have to be very patient. Sometimes the password is not accepted – it functions in the airports of Italy and Germany but not in the USA – and sometimes someone has changed the firewall without telling me. It takes me a long time to find an expert to sort it out, and on top of this I have already lost time tinkering with the system myself.

Time can be frittered away in many different ways. If you don't feel like working, you squander or fritter away your time. You also waste time when you have simply run out of energy. You sit at the computer and make one typing error after another and get no further. Or you are so exhausted you don't feel like going to bed but also can't do anything sensible or take anything in. Others then sit down in front of the television and fritter their time away like that. I just sit and do nothing when I am exhausted. Doing nothing can also be a form of regeneration, or of relaxation in order to be able to go to bed at all. But it is something different from leisure. It is an inability to work and in particular an inability to take advantage of leisure.

Then there is also the kind of slowness resulting from inward resistance to something and avoidance of something that has to be done because you are too involved with your own problems and needs. This lack of self-discipline can turn into idleness. Idleness is the enemy of the soul, says Benedict. You are then a burden on yourself or others.

Of course there is also the kind of dawdling that occurs, for example, when children who are supposed to be getting dressed in the morning don't do anything till mother tells them to hurry up. Children must be taught how to use their time. They must learn that time is something precious. There is nothing to be gained or achieved by squandering time. A mother has to instruct her little boy to tidy up his room. When she comes in after half an hour and nothing has been done then she has to step in and say, "This goes here and that goes there." And when the child says, "I'll do it tomorrow", the answer can only be, "No, it must be done right now!"

Toil is part of life, whether you are big or small. "As long as day lasts we must carry out the work", as it says in the Bible.

Carpe diem, use the time and seize the day. This saying of Horace is not meant hedonistically. But its sense is clear. Use the day because in the evening you can't do anything. Read now, because in the evening it will be too dark to do so. I realized this on a mission station in Africa. I had to go to bed at 8 o'clock after supper and make sure I had got everything done during the daylight. After that it was simply night.

Some people look busy but in reality are frittering away their time. They flit like butterflies from one thing to the next instead of working purposefully. When I was in the Philippines recently it delighted me to see the opposite of this when our young people prepared a feast. They did it in no time at all and afterwards everything was also cleared away again at lightning speed. It was all no trouble, and everything was done with housewifely efficiency.

"I shall guard against two evils today, rushing around and indecision." These words, attributed to John XXIII, imply that we should take care not to be driven and should not squander time. There must be times when people consciously do nothing. This continuous having to do something can become a vice. We must have times when we can switch off, whether by taking a short break or a longer holiday. Switching off doesn't mean just lazing around. This form of idleness is frustrating and boring too. And it is also wasted time.

Disciplined use of time is part of leading a good life. And so is being free of pressure and having leisure in order to be creative.

I am in control if I seek a balance between work and freedom. I can then escape from attempts by others to control me and from the permanent pressure from outside. I do not allow others to exercise power over me. I tackle my work with vigour. But I don't let myself be driven or hurried.

To be irresolute and waste time is just as much of a problem as rushing around. And when I am being either idle or hectic I am not master of my time.

We should be masters of our time, actively shape it and not squander it.

20 Rituals are Necessary

THE following situation occurs repeatedly. Someone comes into my room and stands in front of my desk, which is covered with papers. I have just been working on a report or poring over a file. The person who is standing in front of me wants something urgently. However, I have to keep him waiting, because at this moment the telephone rings. Unfortunately I have to answer it because I can so rarely be reached. And then suddenly the second phone rings and on top of that the mobile phone I have to have which is also on my desk. And meanwhile there's a loud knocking on the door.

In such a situation the only thing to do is keep calm.

First I slowly fill my pipe.

Then I calmly light it.

This is something I deliberately take my time doing.

Afterwards I am available for everyone again.

This for me is a very deliberate ritual. Our day as monks is full of spiritual rituals. But this way of interrupting pressure by slowly filling my pipe has become an additional ritual for me. A secularized ritual. However, I will have to find another ritual, because in the USA I am no longer allowed to smoke anywhere, including in restaurants. So one day there will be nothing for it but to give up smoking altogether. In many places like restaurants and public areas I in any case have no further desire to smoke. Consideration for others apparently has an inhibiting effect on the brain. But sometimes I smile and think how nice it would be nevertheless.

Rituals create a break in the turmoil of everyday life. They take us out of the hustle and bustle around us, give us space and bring us back into the *present.* We make contact with ourselves when we are in danger of getting swept away by the flood of demands on us from outside. Rituals help to make me – and others around me – conscious of the fact that now I first must have some time for myself.

Many suffer because they feel like driftwood, spun helplessly around by external forces. But it has happened when I've complained that it's too much, that I've been told, "It's your own fault", and often enough this is true.

It also can be a form of laziness to allow yourself to be swamped by everything that is going on around you. It requires effort to extract yourself. A deliberately chosen ritual can help prevent you from being just swept along. Self-determined life is *also* a question of time: "time for myself".

Franz von Sales once said you should take an hour a day for prayer. And if you are short of time you should take two hours. Psychologists would call this paradox intervention: deliberate action taken against something that is ruling your life.

Not only prayer but filling a pipe can also be a ritual. It is my own personal ritual, a simple one that helps me to survive. Rituals put up a barrier against the things that are putting pressure on us.

The Divine Office of the monks is an institutionalised form of ritual which helps us centre ourselves in the present. But everyday rituals which everyone can establish are also a way of protecting yourself and giving yourself space to enjoy life. I quite deliberately take time *for* something which does *me* good. I build a safe and protected space around me which signals to myself and others that I am also worth something. I live and am not being lived.

A ritual is a deliberate interruption of pressure. It could be a midday nap, a siesta. A nap in between times is a wonderful ritual. I myself can sleep anywhere, even when it is very loud, or during a bumpy plane ride, or on all kinds of impossible occasions. And a brief nap of this kind is a gift. I enjoy it. Even when it sometimes catches me unawares. Once in St Ottilien on the feast day of the Assumption, when I was sitting on the abbot's throne wearing the mitre, I nodded off repeatedly during the psalms. Someone then wrote to me saying he had seen me dropping off and telling me to take a cold shower before Vespers – which we always celebrate at 2 o'clock in the afternoon, a terrible time. The letter lay on my desk for a long time and I kept coming across it. In the end I did answer it, saying, "You are absolutely right, however I can tell you that I did take a shower beforehand, but it didn't work. Because that evening I wanted to leave at last for a week's holiday, I had worked the whole of the previous night and I was simply dog-tired. I am very sorry that I set you such a bad example."

Rituals not only protect the individual but create a feeling of community. One such ritual, for example, is eating together. Shared rituals have their own particular time structure.

We monks only start eating when everyone has entered the dining hall. Then we stand for prayer. The abbot subsequently signals that we can sit down and start our soup. After the soup we have to wait until he starts the main course. In our prayer we give thanks for the meal and remember everyone to whom we must be grateful that we have enough to eat. As we eat we listen in silence to a reading, and thereby show that we live not only from the gifts of nature but also from the word of God.

In this way we prevent ourselves from eating faster and faster. The abbot finally waits until everyone has finished before he knocks on the table and we stand up for prayer.

During supper, which is normally a little shorter, it can be harder to get the timing right. At the end of the meal we get an apple, and many people just take it with them. Those who however cut and peel it are always behind the others and have to finish eating in a hurry. The abbot or prior then gives the signal for everyone to stand.

The Abbot Primate Benno Gut, the last prince-abbot of Einsiedeln who was later elected as Abbot Primate, was always the last to remove his serviette, so as not to put anyone under pressure. We always tuck our serviettes over the scapular to protect it. The next Abbot Primate was an American who had a different sense of time. He removed his serviette first, and we often still had food on our plates long after he had finished.

The calmness which the previous Abbot Primate emitted was a blessing. We called him not Benno Gut but "Bennone" Gut, a play on the Italian word "bene" and the suffix "one" which reinforces the meaning, because he was such a good person and on no account wanted to put anyone under pressure. Enjoying meals together and waiting for each other is a fine ritual.

When I was archabbot in St Ottilien I aways had guests at my table, including people who were used to talking while eating. They usually also ate much more slowly. With the monks the evening meal at least is always over very quickly, and we finish in eighteen minutes because it is not such a large meal as lunch. One of the guests once said to me, "It's lovely here, but the speed at which you have to eat is almost inhuman." He was right. But if you listen the whole time to a reading, you eat continuously. And those who have finished eating become fidgety. Learning how to wait for others is a very good exercise.

I myself only began the main course when I saw all the others had finished their soup. This much time has to be allowed.

And we usually always waited for our guests. Only if someone was extremely slow would I say, "Please carry on eating afterwards, but we must show consideration to the others." This only happened in exceptional cases. It does us good to take time for meals and allow ourselves and others time.

"Be good to your body, and make your soul want to live in it," says Therese of Avila. Food and drink keep not only body and soul but also a community together. Shared mealtimes enable you to talk to others, share their lives, worries and pleasures and connect you with the others. Eating together is one of the most important rituals in family life, and if it is no longer possible, then the family usually loses some of its solidarity.

Rituals are not only community-oriented, there are also rituals that benefit us on an individual basis, such as jogging or regular exercises.

Movement is also life and movement too needs time. More and more people are taking this time: the woods are full of joggers and in New York they are out on the street. I myself do easy exercises every morning. This is also a type of ritual. I didn't care for sport even at school because I always felt overextended by it. But movement as such simply does you good. I drew up a programme which is not too difficult and is adapted to my situation. I exercise my whole body early in the morning in five to seven minutes. There are stretching exercises for the head and neck, for the upper body, hips and legs. Finally knee bends and a few push-ups and stomach exercises. At the end of them I feel not only fit but simply happy. The day starts differently. If I don't do them, I tire more easily and become sluggish. The knowledge that I feel very good after these physical exercises motivates me to do them even though I may still be dog-tired when I get up. They have become a ritual which I don't want to miss. Afterwards I take a shower – three times hot and cold – and then go to church for the first prayers.

However, I don't want to be too rigid about all this. The joggers who no longer run out of doors but only on treadmills in fitness centres are a phenomenon that is peculiar to our time. But even they are doing themselves good by taking time for themselves. I am convinced that after a certain time they feel better.

Of course there are many people who torment themselves so that they can eat more again afterwards. These however are more the people who go to the sauna and then down several beers. One fellow monk, a professor in Rome, always cycled from Rome to Ostia every Thursday on his day off, in order to lose weight. At his destination he always ate a huge portion of spaghetti. When he told me this I smiled. But that is all right too.

Rituals give structure to our lives. We don't just trifle away our time and a day doesn't just "run away with us" if we for example plan times of meditation. If we sit down and think about the day instead of sleeping in front of the telly. And if we as it were offer the day to God and ask His pardon if something has gone wrong, this is ultimately liberating. Establishing a ritual instead of dozing away the remainder of the day not only gives shape to the day, it also gives our time meaning.

We need rituals. Even if it is only the way I fill my pipe. Even when some people accuse me of setting a bad example. I deal calmly with such reproaches.

Someone once wrote to me that he had thought so highly of me, also because of the hospitals I had built. But when he saw a photo of me with a pipe it had destroyed his positive image of me. I would also die sooner and cost the state a lot of money.

To this gentleman I wrote that I understood his concerns and I was admittedly a weak person, but I wanted to remind him that he would cost the state just as much. Because he didn't smoke, he would live to be over ninety and the state would have to pay out a lot of pension money for him . . .

I thought I wouldn't hear from him again. But I did. He replied that he would think about what I'd said.

Well, at least that, I thought.

21 Time to Dream and Time to Grow

GROWTH and maturity are not simultaneous processes. As we can see from children, education also takes time. "What I expect from a reform of our education system is that the students will have time to put their feet on the table, stare at the ceiling and dream." I have shocked not a few teachers with this statement. When I am addressing educationalists about school problems or reforms I repeatedly come back to this point. My ideas of a proper education and social etiquette differ from those of a lot of people. But especially at a time when they are being put under pressure from all directions, it cannot be said enough that children need time to grow up. The biblical proverb is equally applicable to them: growing has its own time. Every period in life has its own time and every period must be seen positively. Respect for children and respect for life demands this. Only if we remove the constant pressure from them can they become creative human beings. And it is precisely this, promoting the creative potential, that is the purpose of a good upbringing and school, and is what our society needs.

A young journalist was recently talking about being

a new father. He had a little daughter called Vera who was just ten months old and taking her first steps. She was so charming and was already trying to talk and bouncing on her mother's lap to the songs of Madonna.

Nevertheless, her father is already worried about her future. He is already looking at nursery schools, preschools and schools where his little girl might go later on. While she is still shouting with glee, and is *joie de vivre* in person, her parents are already hatching plans and thinking about her future career, mapping out her life and future. And by this means they are building up the pressure.

But life is not plannable. And children's lives even less so. I find it terrible that parents want to programme so far ahead and consult experts for the purpose, that they are trying to create "ideal children" into whom they project their own ideas. I feel really angry when parents force their own wishes and fantasies on their children and – to cite an example that is not even particularly extreme – try to genetically manipulate a child who might perhaps have become a musician and turn him into a boxer instead. How would I react if others had made decisions for me and my life in this way?

But it is not only parents who programme children. Politicians in section "U3" of the education field are seriously drawing up programmes for children from birth up until the age of three. At this stage they are to be made fit "for life". What this means is that they should be able to earn a living later on. This has all the characteristics of a planned economy – a system that is designed purely to provide efficient education and make sure that the "human capital" is invested as quickly as possible in the economy.

I prefer the Indian proverb, which is also closer to life and says that grass grows no faster when you pull at it.

Even children who grow up in our modern society need values other than those of efficiency and fast learning. They need play and fantasy, fairytales and free time. Of course there are other needs too: diligence, discipline, perseverance, resilience and fairness.

For all this children need time: to practise the relevant skills, to enjoy life, to develop their personalities and to grow up to be happy people.

The modern education system with its full timetables and rapid succession of curricula prevents children from being really creative. It's not an education system, it's a training system. At a conference I attended on the future of the school, a prime minister spoke repeatedly of education and the need for education reform. I asked, "What is really the matter here? It's funny, since the nineteen-sixties we've had one education reform after the other, but our children are allegedly becoming more and more stupid. However, the humanistic education we had by no means left us intellectual cripples." Then it was pointed out to me that the politician was not speaking about education, what he meant was training reforms. But our choice of words betrays us.

A climate of competition amongst children prevents them from developing creative potential. Children are curious and open for everything that surrounds them when they are allowed to be. They *want* to be creative, but in their own time. And not under pressure to perform by economically obsessed education politicians or well-meaning but primarily ambitious parents, who cart even nursery school children from piano lessons to ballet or Chinese classes.

I myself have realized while practising music that when I always have to learn new pieces of music and as soon as one concert is over already have to start preparing for the next one, then I have no time left for improvisation. I don't have time to listen to the sounds properly or practise a few runs on the flute that particularly interest me. The lack of time is like a lack of air. Then I have no more air and become breathless. Breathlessness: that is the main obstacle to real perfection.

Children need freedom. When I hear that today creative management is part of education, I can only say, forget it! Creativity can't be ground out like minced meat, it can't be "produced". It can only grow when it is given time to do so. That is our problem: we always want to be able to produce everything. But creativity can't be manufactured, otherwise it is no longer creativity. It is precisely for this reason that children must sometimes be allowed to be lazy and to play, and must have time to dream. They need the protective zone of times when they can do what they want.

Knowledge crammed in like fast food blocks the imagination and hinders creativity. It is in addition not properly digested and soon forgotten. It inhibits or hampers natural curiosity. Maturity and growth require an atmosphere of freedom. Here potential of a quite different kind can be developed. "We are such stuff as dreams are made on." When we dream, we step outside the many practical concerns which hedge us about every day. In dreams, including daydreams when we fantasize or allow our minds to wander, we are also closer to our souls. We can give free rein to our longings and innermost wishes. It is another kind of wakefulness. Here our inner liveliness and inner richness are activated because we are not just having to react to stimuli or impulses from outside. We should allow children to give their imagination free rein and encourage their innate abilities. This is also incidentally the best way of immunizing them against misuse as the economic tools of a performance-oriented society.

If children have time when no demands are being made of them, then they are better protected from the danger of passive escape to the television and computer. A clever child psychologist called the television and computer "child catchers". They work on children just like those sticky fly catchers where the victims stick even faster the more they try to wriggle free.

The richer the inner world of a person is, the safer he is from manipulation. Someone with a lively imagination is able to see the world not only as it is, but as it ought to be. The ability to dream is thus much more than simple wishing. The imagination doesn't create an ideal world or a false reality, but helps people to measure and define the distance between what is and what could be. And this is the mark of a creative person.

This is why it is so important that children are read stories and fairytales. Stories help children to learn how to master reality.

This skill is also activated through play. I have thus always argued that the children at our monastery school should have enough time for music, games and sport. Also for playing football, which is healthy and has a toughening aspect. It has rules and enables the children to practise social behaviour. As students we used to secretly play cards during art lessons. Even cards teach you life skills. Card players practise arithmetic when they count up how many trumps the other players have in their hands. They learn how to see through things and think ahead. They practise taking risks and learn how not to get duped. And have fun in the process.

When children need freedom *and* structure, protection *and* adventure, new experiences *and* continuity, then the adults have to be prepared to give them their time. Time is required if children are to receive the attention they need from parents and teachers: this much is clear. This too promotes creativity in perhaps the most natural way. By paying children attention, teachers or parents bring out what they have in them.

Children know very well when the adults themselves have such full timetables and are under such pressure that they have no leisure and no free time to do exactly what they want.

That is why we adults need to set children an example. By demonstrating that there is a life beyond obsession with performance, we show them that it is necessary to take time and allow oneself the freedom to live rather than be pushed through life. Children who have experienced this will later be better able to live an independent life in which frequent changes will be unavoidable.

I recently read an interview with the head of CERN, the famous nuclear research centre in Geneva. He said, "I became a physicist because the person who taught me physics was a great person and a great teacher." And one of the best known German actresses, Brigitte Hobmeier, recently confessed in an interview in the Süddeutsche Zeitung that it was the encouragement of a teacher that enabled her to want to become an actress and go to drama school. She came from a background where acting was only thinkable as a hobby, if at all. It was this teacher, she said, who had prevented her from being unable to think she could make acting her career.

Nowadays it is important to focus more on this kind of influence. It is only from people and from daily examples that children will be taught what they most need to learn: how to live.

That is why I will continue to take every opportunity to attack the hasty, rapidly implemented education reforms which are imposed on children, teachers and parents at increasingly shorter intervals by so-called "education" bureaucrats.

Children thus need time, and they need it now. Free

time without schedules, without performance requirements and without learning goals. And that is why I am happy for every child who puts his feet on the table and dreams.

22 Values – Attitudes for Life

"AND lead us not into temptation" – we all know this sentence in the Lord's Prayer. We are also familiar with certain kinds of headlines in the papers. Someone allows himself to be celebrated as a super manager who is only thinking of the common good and setting a good example. And then it comes to light that he has evaded taxes on an inconceivable scale. A trade union is negotiating with an airline and the head of the trade union flies to an exotic destination with a free ticket from this airline which he had obtained in his official capacity as a member of its supervisory board, instead of staying to support his union members in this critical situation. There are fine words from a company boss and a few months later they are worthless because certain things have become public which should never have been revealed. These people set themselves up as examples and promptly succumbed to temptation.

But we must be careful: we mustn't start sermonizing! First there is the hope that they will reform, and, let's be honest, how many of us would have resisted temptation in a similar situation? How many of us would not also seize a favourable opportunity if it presented itself? The sentence from the Lord's Prayer applies to all of us. The Christian image of man is honest: man is a sinner. Trust is good, control is not necessarily better but is also to some extent appropriate as a form of security. We need ideals, of that there is no question. But we should not overestimate ourselves. Values cannot be instilled by means of a crash course.

Even the monks of ancient times knew that pure saints were rare. People became saints because they resisted temptation and in this way became stronger. The Father of all Monks, Anthony, once said that temptation strengthens the monk in the same way as a tree puts its roots down deeper into the earth when it is shaken by a storm. If we want to be steadfast, we must have moral strength. This takes a long time to acquire and requires perseverance, practice and interaction with others.

We all need to help each other every day through example, awareness and attention. Partners must provide each other with this support in a marriage and parents must help their children. In society the weak must be helped by the strong. It is no different at school. Education is something that in the long run helps the young to lead good, moral lives.

Moral strength as a spiritual quality which affects our actions is something that only becomes second nature through practice and perseverance over a long period of time. We can organize as many ethics lessons as we want, we can describe the classic catalogue of virtues from a historical and systematic point of view and explain their relevance: prudence, courage, justice, modesty and anything else we want to include. It's all very plausible. But why doesn't it have an immediate effect? And why does the majority not make an effort to practise these virtues? Because the majority is weak, all of us are weak.

In our order, in the monasteries, it is the daily routine, the rhythm followed throughout life which finally becomes second nature. Only when I regularly get up at 6 o'clock in the morning can I stick to the rhythm of a monastic day. And it is the same for everybody.

Education is also not just quickly hammering in material prescribed by the curriculum. The children must be encouraged to be good, so that goodness becomes second nature, consciousness of values becomes an *attitude* that takes effect in everyday life and becomes an *inner strength* when temptation comes in certain situations. We are all creatures of habit. Becoming good does not happen from one moment to the next. We need constant practice, constant reminders of what does good and is important.

Of course it is useful to test vocabulary regularly at school and repeatedly check the students' level of knowledge. We all know what knowledge young people should have, what they should be taught about history or economic realities or what they should be taught so they can master a language. But that is not what I mean by education in values. This is primarily accustoming children to goodness. And this takes a long time and needs perseverance.

The way to happiness always involves renunciation and

patience. People have to be encouraged and motivated. Here it is important not to always take the line of least resistance. This is a general principle but it applies particularly to children. They have to learn to make an effort. Parents and teachers are not doing children a favour if they do not make demands of them. My mother didn't know a word of Latin, but she forced me in the evening to learn my vocabulary and in the morning before I got up she sat by my bed and tested me. Then I could go to school.

When we have gone through something together, we will grow. A crisis weathered jointly will bind people together. Surviving problems in a marriage strengthens the relationship. It is an essential part of a friendship to stand by one another in difficult times. Musicians have to struggle with the "dead tone" and practise, practise, practise before they get anywhere. Anyone who has ever played an instrument or learned a language knows that you have periods when you don't seem to progress at all. Later on it is a wonderful feeling not to have given up in spite of everything. Only then, in sport too, when we keep on repeating our achievement and persevere with our practising without giving up do we develop resilience. Life means being able to endure things. You learn as a young person how to clench your teeth. And that is what we must expect of the young.

Discipline is important. The principles are really quite simple. Children come home from school and should first do their homework and then be allowed to play. But no, what a lot of parents say is, the poor boy, he's had such a full morning, we can't expect him to sit down and work. So the boy goes off to play and doesn't come back, or if he does, he picks up his Game Boy. This is all very understandable. I still have to discipline myself today when I am constantly being distracted from my work with all kinds of requests. Then the only thing I can do is close the door and say now I've got some peace and can attend first to the things I really should have been doing. How will our children later be able to deal with all the various stimuli of life today if they haven't learned discipline?

There are other subjects which are not in the curriculum. One of them is honesty. Is this still an officially accepted virtue? No-one tells the truth to the powerful managing board of a major corporation. Even members of managing boards admit to me that no-one dares to be straight with them. That is *really* sad. *That* is what we have to work against, starting at school.

And then there is fair play. This is what children learn when they play football. They practise how to win honestly and lose decently. Learn how not to go over the top when they win and not flip out when they lose.

Children need models who teach them how to grow up to be independent, value-conscious human beings. The real purpose of school is not swotting up masses of material but rather learning, and wanting to learn to see reality critically and alertly. This is the only way to become immune against all ideologies. Greek lessons did not give us a language we could use for communicating today in our global and polyglot world. But our Greek teacher nevertheless taught us to think when we read Socrates' dialogues. We did not understand very much, but nevertheless learned how to make distinctions. This Socrates kept on asking until a term was defined and did not let the other person go until it had been established what was really meant.

And we should not, finally, exclude religion from education. Religion for many people is just one way of looking at life, and Christianity is the one out of the many which they would most like to eliminate from public life in a pluralistic society. Religion is an established part of our lives. We must not allow it to be restricted to Sunday and excluded from daily life. The secular life has its own laws and is in conflict with religion. But religion gives a deeper meaning to life. We must not withhold this truth from our children. It will also take courage in the future to educate our children in religion. Healthy spirituality does not lead to suppression, but to freedom and joy in life.

In religious education, values have a particular basis. Religion is not just a school subject. Religious education should wake the students up, it should make them conscious of our relationship with God and the fact that we are created beings, conscious of our frailty and our limitations as human beings. It should be directed against an image of humanity where everything is possible and an ideology which says I am in control, I am the author of my being. Religious education is missing the point if it only serves to impart information.

Our society is obsessed by feasibility mania. Only things that can be done quickly are valuable. Everything is apparently possible. But the actual principle of basic Christian values is that everything is not available to us, derived from our understanding of our world and of man as the creation of God. To accept this and find orientation, must we learn all over again how to be humble? Is it simply humble to behave in this way, to ask what does the creation tell us? What is the correct attitude? The philosopher Paul Feyerabend introduced the principle which governed and endangered a whole generation: anything goes, everything is allowed. Although this can be understood in a positive sense, as rebellion against ideological rigidity, it is also true that everything has its limitations and its predefined laws.

There are also limitations imposed on us by nature, which it is dangerous for us to exceed. To realize and accept these limitations must become second nature from childhood on. This is something which we must make young people aware of. Our life and our world is a gift we cannot do what we want with.

A value-oriented education is thus not just limited to the school timetable, parental upbringing or instruction in religion. It is the *permanent* duty of the whole society. A society in which the honest people are the stupid ones and the motto is don't get caught, passes this message on to the next generation. There must once again be a goal for all of us. What do we really want? What should our society be like? A child must already learn at home that honesty is the best policy and that the goal of living together is not to hoodwink everyone else.

What I wish for myself and all of us is that our future society will still have values and be determined by what is good. Attributes such as diligence and perseverance are important. But there are other values as well which are exemplified by the divine virtues: fidelity, compassion, patience, forgiveness and above all love. Goodness should be carried on into our future. This is the only way society can survive.

What does all this have to do with time? A great deal! Transmitting values in education is not something that can be done in a few hours at school. Values have to be lived on an everyday basis and permanently internalized. We adults, whatever our station in life, must stick to our values in the family, in schools, in our jobs, so that the young catch on. All of us, without exception, must help with this.

Values can be inconvenient. To make a habit of them is a lifelong task that falls to us every day.

23 Grateful Every Day

ON my last birthday I was away. I was working on something with other people and someone asked me whether this day was special for me. I replied, "Yes and no." And it is really the case that since I have become older I think more often about the past. And I tend more to ask myself certain questions: Where have you got to exactly, what do you think of your life when you take stock? What has come out of your original life plan?

Usually I do not brood too long and I soon direct my attention back to the here and now. What have I got to do next? What have I got to do tomorrow?

Even though such questions are important, I know that not much is going to change. Especially when you look back over long stretches of your life, you realize how little you have really changed.

On a day like my birthday, however, I tell myself very deliberately that I am very grateful. I am grateful for the way my life has gone. When I eventually die I will know my life was never boring. Gratitude is for me the heart of spirituality. Gratitude for being alive at all, and for being able to accept one's whole life and to see everything as a gift. Everything, including my time, is a gift.

For this reason a birthday is also an opportunity to pause and take time out from the hectic activity of the day. This does not however only apply to a special day like this, but to every day.

The person who is grateful cannot be hectic because a grateful person pauses. And it is only then that you are able to experience gratitude.

I am grateful at very specific moments, such as when I sit in an Alpine meadow and think oh Lord, how beautiful it is here! What a blessing that I can be here, thank you.

I once experienced a moment in my everyday life when I felt particularly blessed. The person in the car in front of me on the motorway was driving so dangerously that I had to drive over a verge marker to avoid him. A tyre burst and the car spun right round. When we came to a stop and were able to get out of the car unhurt I said, "First I need a cigar." When the policeman who arrived on the scene saw me he could only shake his head and say, "Well, you can't have had too much of a shock if you can already smoke." I replied, "Why should I have had?"

It was something else.

The knowledge that I am in God's hands gives me a basic calmness which is important for my life. This is a freedom which comes from faith. When I get in a car or on a plane I cross myself. Whatever might happen, I am not anxious.

Whatever happens, everything has its time. Everything is ultimately safe in God and for this I am grateful.

I never say this was God's plan. Determinism is not what I believe in. No, I think the opposite is true. If I must make a comparison, what I feel is more like the trust of a child in his father. I know that, whatever happens, I am in God's hands. He will look after me.

We can even be grateful for the bad things we have experienced in life. Not because they were bad, but because the way we survived them ultimately made us more mature. They challenged us and enabled us to progress, and thus had their own important function.

"If you possess all the happiness in the world but don't look on it as a gift then it will not give you any pleasure. But even misfortune will give joy to those who are able to be grateful for it." The author of these words, the Austrian Benedictine monk, David Steindl-Rast, isn't saying we should be fatalistic in the sense of accepting everything as it is, and saying nothing can be done about it.

Gratitude means something different. It is a simple yes. I say yes to my life wholeheartedly but I don't see it as blind fate. Through gratitude, life and all it involves is lifted on to a personal plane. Fate is something negative. It represents submission to something I do not understand, to blind fate. Fate has nothing to do with personality. Gratitude is a personal matter. I can be grateful to a person, but not to a fate.

Perhaps it is something to do with humility?

Humility and gratitude are related. To be grateful to somebody requires an element of modesty. Humility doesn't mean submissiveness. I am prepared to accept my life as "given", as a gift of which I was not the author.

Gratitude also has something to do with allowing things to happen and calmness. The Greek word "charis" comes closest to it: grace or blessings which are bestowed on us.

It certainly does not just mean hope for calm and settled times. Qohelet writes that "There is a time to kill, a time for war, and a time for peace." I can look at this positively and say there are times when I have to work really hard and there are times of rest. I cannot be only idle or only resting. I am grateful for both.

We are not the author of everything, the author is the Holy Spirit. When I realize this I can once again look at things calmly and see where we really are doing something wrong.

Gratitude for everything that is does not mean remaining passive. It means being open for everything the Holy Spirit is planning with me. Listening to "What the Spirit is telling his communities" (Revelations 2) implies not inactivity, but a vibrant response.

This also means that I work, try to listen and question everything if necessary. Not in order to criticize but to make a "human" reservation. Perhaps it was only human after all while all the time I was thinking it was divine.

Thanks be to God – for this reservation too.

24 Bless Your Time

SUBIACO, a small town in the Latium region near Rome, became famous because St Benedict dwelt in solitude here. Sacro speco, the holy cave in which he lived, is painted with beautiful frescos. If I am in the area I always visit this place. When you walk down the steps in this cave you suddenly see two fascinating scenes on each side of you, which were probably intended as Biblia pauperum, visual teaching aids.

The right-hand picture shows Death the horseman with his followers. He is stabbing at a young couple enjoying life and hunting with falcons. Behind him are people who are sick and old and want to die but are unable to, begging desperately for death.

The picture on the opposite side shows a monk. He is depicted with three young people and here too the reality is made clear: one person who has just died is laid out in a coffin. In a second coffin the body has worms crawling in it while in a third one, finally, only the bones are to be seen. It makes a very strong impression.

For me this cycle of illustrations embodies a deep truth, which never loses its relevance: none of us know when death will come. Neither those who are living life to the full nor those who are tired of living. So often do we find ourselves standing speechless at the grave of a young person. The wealth of this splendidly dressed young couple who are hunting with falcons is no use to them. It shows only too clearly how fast everything can disappear. *Media in vita*, in the midst of the life they – we – are surrounded by death.

That is the wisdom of the Old Testament. "Our life fades like a shadow" (Ps 144:4). Nobody knows his time. And the New Testament says much the same thing, that time is not in our hands.

When I see this scene with the rich young couple in Subiaco, I also think of a parable of Jesus: of the rich man who is building a new barn to store his wealth in ignorance of the fact that he will not live to see the next day. For the super-rich of our day who are constantly looking for ways of investing their money so that it will continue to increase, for all the top managers who are always after more, as if they did not already have enough, the same applies: this night your life could be over. What then is really enduring? What is really worth anything?

What real values are was shown me once by an elderly woman who said to me at her husband's grave, "You know, everything is ultimately borrowed, all the material goods and even our lives themselves." This attitude is a sign of maturity. There is no way of acquiring this attitude, unless by repeatedly stopping and thinking what things are really worth, such as our possessions and titles, and what we are worth to ourselves and to others.

Someone who can say at the end of his life, "I have lived my life. It is meant to be", has dignity. I experienced this with my own father. It was in 1992 when I visited him for the last time. I was in Neu-Ulm for a confirmation and had to fly next day to Israel, as Dormition Abbey wanted to join our Congregation. It was my first visit to the Holy Land. I said to myself, before I set off I'll look in on my parents. At some point one of them will no longer be there when I come back from one of my many trips. My father was lying on the sofa, wrapped up in a blanket and very cheerful. When it was time for me to leave and I said goodbye he said, "We're not going to see each other again." I replied, "Father, don't talk nonsense." But he insisted, "My life is coming to an end." "How come?" I asked, and he replied, "Why should I continue to live? All these doctors' consultations are pointless. I have done what I needed to in my life and you children have done well. Take care of your mother when I am no longer there." Then we said goodbye. It was Whit Monday, and before I flew on Tuesday I spoke to him once more on the telephone. Everything was fine. On Wednesday his condition deteriorated and on Thursday he was admitted to hospital. On Friday I called from Tel Aviv before I flew back to find out how he was. He was just having a CT examination. When I landed in Frankfurt he was dead.

He knew. He was almost eighty-six when he passed away. When he received the last rites he said, "Well, now

I've made it." It's the sort of thing you might say after successfully finishing an important job. What grace to have all you want out of life and be able to say goodbye peacefully. To leave the world with such cheerfulness was the greatest gift my father gave me. This was how he felt. He said yes – and blessed his time.

To bless the time means to relinquish life in peace. When I say yes to my mortality and to death, I bless my time and am at peace with my life, I cope serenely with my finiteness. I am reconciled to it.

As far as the relationship to death is concerned, there is a difference whether you say, "It's over, that was it", or whether your life is not definitively over and swept away like debris. There is a difference whether you see the end of life as absolute and definite or whether you believe that your own finite being is merged into the eternity of God. Hope is saying, my worldly life is finished but that is not the end. My life is in the hands of God. And because my life is not in my hands but in His I can remain calm.

Recently Inge Jens, the wife of the philosopher and author Walter Jens who is suffering from Alzheimer's, was interviewed by the magazine *Stern*. She said, "I am someone who has lost her partner. The man I loved no longer exists." The disease had transformed her husband into another person. "He is no longer my husband." In the book "Dying with dignity", which Walter Jens wrote together with the theological professor Hans Küng, he argues in favour of active euthanasia. In the last discussions he was able to hold he apparently complained that animals are put to sleep, but not people. "But he missed the right moment to put an end to his life in the truest sense of the word", said Inge Jens in the magazine interview. I found this shocking. Instead of talking about how much love she is giving him . . . What kind of attitude is it when someone with Alzheimer's threatens to commit suicide and the people who love him think this is right, because he is no longer in control of himself and this is no longer dignified?

We are all afraid of losing control. But this is what real Christian humility is about: relinquishing control. And this is exactly why euthanasia goes against the tenets of Christianity. Because in the Christian view an Alzheimer's patient is also a valuable person. When I read that assisted suicide is seriously discussed and that in Holland granny can be dispatched during the week so that the family is not disturbed at the weekend, and that the former Minister of Justice of Hamburg has presented an injection machine to an old age home so that people can dispose of themselves, I find it very morbid.

All this is part of the desire to be fully in charge of your own time and of yourself and not to have to accept your finiteness. Benedict XVI is quite rightly always talking about this. People no longer want to be created beings, they want in an infantile way to be their own master.

It is not always easy to imagine dying in peace. But this not only has a long tradition with the monks, there is also something human about it. There is a story of an old monk who after a long life was on his deathbed in the Egyptian desert, with his brethren gathered around him in sorrow. He, however, opened his eyes and laughed. And he did this a second and a third time. The brothers asked in astonishment, "Abbas, why you are laughing when we are weeping?" He replied, "The first time I laughed was because you all fear death. The second time it was because you are not prepared to die and the third time because I am going from work to rest."

It is understandable to want to die peacefully. A confrere who had been bedridden for a long time called me to his sickbed when he felt that he was going to die. He said, "The doctor has just been and has diagnosed a femoral neck fracture. He wants to admit me to hospital. Please prevent it, because even if it heals, with my osteoporosis, my leg will break again somewhere else. I want to be able to die with my brothers around me."

Of course I respected his wish. When life is at an end then it is at an end. And when somebody has had all he wants out of life then it is also something beautiful.

At the end of his life, St Martin of Tours said, "*Non recuso laborem* – Lord if I am still needed by your people, I refuse no work or travail. Thy will be done." He was returning to his monastery from a peace mission when his strength left him and his fellow monks asked him not to desert them. But his hour had come and "he gave his spirit back to heaven", as Simplicius Severus tells us.

Death is not a tragedy. With God there is no time. Everyone is there with God at the same time. Some people who lose a loved one say, "I wish I had died before him." I can understand this very well. But I am certain that we all come to God at the same time. He knows no time. Because in this eternal way He is turned towards us all then I am connected with all people.

Sometimes I am very tired myself, tired of living in that sense that I say, "Lord I would also like to be able to sleep." Or it sometimes happens that at 1 o'clock in the morning I say, "Must this go on forever, can't I have my peace?"

Then someone smiles down from up there and says "Carry on," and this gives me strength.

The most important thing is to live life with calmness, conscientiousness but also with serenity and say, "I cannot do everything, and when it is time others should replace me."

Life is beautiful – in spite of all its trouble and stress.

But I am ready at any time to accept that it is at an end.

And when I die then I will say, now others should continue.

And if it is not yet to be – then I will go on, in God's name.